LATIN COURSE

Part

By L. A. Wilding
LATIN COURSE FOR SCHOOLS, PART I
LATIN COURSE FOR SCHOOLS, PART II
LATIN COURSE FOR SCHOOLS, PART III
GREEK FOR BEGINNERS

By R. W. L. Wilding
KEY TO LATIN COURSE FOR SCHOOLS, PART I
KEY TO LATIN COURSE FOR SCHOOLS, PART II
KEY TO LATIN COURSE FOR SCHOOLS, PART III

LATIN COURSE FOR SCHOOLS

Part 1

by

L. A. WILDING, M.A.

Senior Classical Master, Dragon School, Oxford
Late Assistant Master St. Edward's School
Formerly Scholar of Oriel College, Oxford

THIRD EDITION

FABER AND FABER LIMITED

London, Boston

First published in 1949
by Faber and Faber Limited
3 Queen Square London W.C.1
Second edition revised and enlarged 1952
Reprinted 1954
This edition revised and enlarged 1955
Reprinted 1957, 1958, 1960, 1962, 1965,
1968, 1972, 1975, 1978 and 1981
Printed and bound in Great Britain by
Redwood Burn Limited
Trowbridge & Esher
All rights reserved

ISBN 0 571 06517 1

Preface to the Third Edition

Additional exercises, graded according to the chapters, have been printed at the end of this edition to provide further practice in translating and composing Latin sentences.

Oxford, 1954

Preface to the Second Edition

Apart from some corrections, the only change in the second edition is the inclusion of lists of the more common Latin words at the end of the book. The lists correspond to the chapters, and it is suggested that they will be found useful for revision, as a basis for tests, and for the invention of further examples.

Oxford, 1952

Preface to the First Edition

There seems to be room for yet another attempt to present the first stages of Latin. The successful covering of this ground must inevitably depend upon the resources of the teacher, and though this book is not offered as a substitute for these resources, it is framed in the hope that it will fit in with them, and also save him or her much time spent in the invention of examples.

The Grammar and rules of elementary Syntax are presented in an ordered sequence, and within this framework the book is planned in the hope that the pupil may feel from the beginning both a sense of achievement and a genuine interest in the language and subject-matter. Care has been taken not to bewilder him by the premature use of any forms that have not already been explained: on this principle, for example, the Adjective is not introduced until it can be fully declined, i.e. until the neuter Noun has been reached.

Latin precedes English both in the expositions of Grammar and Syntax, chapter by chapter, and in the exercises throughout the book. Emphasis is thus laid upon Latin as a medium of thought.

Although forms and rules must be unfolded in isolated sentences in the first instance, most teachers agree that continuous translation should be begun at once, even if there is some difficulty in providing natural Latin in continuity, within the confines of the first few grammatical forms. A few of the continuous pieces in this book are made up, most of them are adapted. The subject-matter deals mainly with Roman Britain and early Roman history (both illustrated by maps). Roman Britain has been chosen because of its immediate appeal and in the hope that its inclusion will lead to a further interest in the subject and to visits to any Roman remains that are accessible; the episodes from early Roman history are exciting in themselves, and help to illustrate some of the old Roman virtues.

The *sources*, therefore, are mainly Caesar, Tacitus, and Livy. There are one or two side-glances at Greek history, in the hope that the pupil may be helped, even at this stage, to realise the unity of the civilisations of Greece and Rome. The vocabulary is fairly large, but (i) words are often repeated, (ii) nearly all the words are ones which the pupil will soon meet again, (iii) the pupil not only meets the conventional examples as *grammar*, but uses nearly all of them in translation.

Almost from the beginning there are included pieces of continuous English for translation into Latin, founded upon the Latin-English pieces which precede them. It has been suggested that this early introduction of Latin *Proses* will be helpful and obviate some of the difficulties that are often presented by a sudden transition to prose at a later stage. They may, of course, be omitted at the discretion of the teacher.

The Grammar covered by this book is as follows (the Syntax being founded upon its simpler uses): the Indicative, Imperative, and Infinitive of the four Conjugations (Active only) and of **sum**; the five Declensions; the main types of Adjectives; Common Pronouns (including Reflexive) and Prepositions; a few Adverbs and Conjunctions. The Passive Voice is purposely left until Part II.

I am much indebted for constructive suggestions to Mr. R. H. Barrow, Mr. A. E. Lynam, Mr. R. St. J. Yates, and Mr. S. C. Crowther-Smith, to none of whom, however, are due any shortcomings that the book may contain; I am most grateful to Mr. F. E. Hicks for the two maps, and to Mr. J. B. Poynton for helpful corrections both of the manuscript and of the proofs.

Oxford, 1949

Introduction to the Beginner

The study of a foreign language is an exciting matter; it is like a key that will open many doors. By it we can read the literature of another people, and learn their ways of life, their history, and their thoughts; we can talk to the people whose language it is, and come to a greater understanding of them.

How does this apply to the study of Latin?

(1) By a knowledge of Latin we are introduced to a great people, the Romans. The Romans led the world as men of action; they built good roads, made good laws, and organised what was in their time almost world-wide government and citizenship. At their best, too, they set the highest examples of honour, loyalty and self-sacrifice. The Romans wrote of their own achievements in a noble language, and, fortunately, a large amount of what they wrote, both in prose and in poetry, has survived.

One reason, then, for learning Latin is the study of a practical people who have given many good things to our own civilisation and have expressed themselves in a literature that is always stately and often beautiful.

Britain was occupied by the Romans from A.D. 43 to A.D. 410, and there are few parts of the country from which Roman remains of some kind cannot easily be reached; most museums have an interesting Roman section. For these reasons, the pieces of Latin in the earlier part of this book deal with Roman Britain. Later on, there are some of the more exciting stories of the early Romans in Italy. Because the story of the Roman civilisation is part of one big story which includes the story of the Greeks, there are also in this book some pieces of Latin about people who were famous in Greek history or legend.

(2) Latin is not today a spoken language, but owing to the influence of Rome, there are traces of Latin in every sentence we speak. There are more words in the English language that come from Latin than from any other source, and a study of

Latin gives us a knowledge of the real meaning of many of the words we use. Latin, then, is a key to our own language.

(3) Another very important point is that the Romans both thought and expressed themselves with the utmost clearness. One of the chief objects of education is to learn how to express ourselves clearly, and there is no better way of reaching this goal than by studying Latin.

To sum it up, we do not go abroad to find people who speak this language. Latin lies deep down in us all, in the civilisation of which we are members, in our laws and system of government, in our cities and in our very speech. If we go back to Latin itself, we shall be better able to understand what we have grown up from and what we live for, and our ways of thinking will grow clearer.

This book has been written to introduce you to Latin in the simplest possible way; the more you learn of Latin and of the Romans, the more you will find that what is written above is true.

Note on the Latin Alphabet

The Latin Alphabet corresponds to the English alphabet, except that it has no J, U, or W, and Y and Z only come in words borrowed from Greek.

The letter I was used both as a Vowel and as a Consonant (pronounced as *y* in *yes*), e.g. **Iūlius**, in which both uses of this letter are seen. In some books Consonant -I is written as **J**, e.g. **Jūlius**.

V was used both as our Vowel U and as a Consonant (pronounced like English *w*), but nowadays the vowel is always written as a U, e.g. in **Valerius**.

K is only found rarely, e.g. **Kalendae**.

In all oral work care should be taken to give vowels their correct quantity.

Contents

Every chapter contains exercises from Latin into English and from English into Latin. The following is a summary of the Grammar and Syntax covered by each chapter, with the titles of the pieces of continuous Latin Translation.

12 *Contents*

14 *Contents*

MAPS

Chapter 1

The Verb: 1st Conjugation, Present Indicative Active

The study of the **Verb** comes first, because it is from the Verb that we get the chief clues to the meaning of any Latin sentence.

Every Latin Verb has a **Stem** or main body: this Stem gives the *general meaning* of the Verb.

Here are the Stems of some Latin Verbs, with their *general meanings*:

nāvigā-	*sail.*	labōrā-	*work.*
explōrā-	*spy out.*	aedificā-	*build.*
superā-	*conquer.*	arā-	*plough.*

If we come across a piece of Latin which contains the six Verbs of which these are the Stems, we can get a clue to the *general meaning* of the piece. We can easily imagine an account of somebody going overseas and getting busy in a colony. This information will be supplied by the meanings of the Stems.

But the *general meaning* is not enough. We want to know:

(1) The **Number** of people who do the various things. Is it one or more?

(2) The **Person** (or Persons) who do them. Is it *I* (or *we*), *you* (singular or plural), *he* or *she* or *it* (or *they*)?

(3) The **Time** of the action. Is it *sail*, *will sail*, or *were sailing*, etc.?

(4) Whether the person or persons in the story *conquer* somebody else or are themselves *conquered* by somebody else. If they *are conquered*, it makes all the difference to the story! In the same way do *they build* houses, or *had* houses *already been built*?

All these questions are answered by the **Verb Endings** which are joined to the Stem.

Here is an example of an Ending joined to a Stem: the result gives us a definite part of a Verb with an *exact meaning*:

Stem	Ending	Part of Verb	Exact Meaning
amā-	-mus	amā-mus[1]	*we love, are loving,*
(general meaning,		amāmus	*do love.*
love)			

[1] The hyphen is only put in to make clear how the definite part of the Verb is formed; we do not use hyphens in writing Latin.

Verb Endings: four clues

If we examine **amā-mus** closely, we find that the ending gives us four clues to the *exact meaning* of the word, once we know that the *general meaning* of the Stem **amā-** is *love*:

(1) The **Number** of people, of whom the statement **amāmus** is made, is more than one, i.e. is Plural (not Singular).

(2) The **Person** is 1st Person (not 2nd or 3rd).

(3) The Time of the action of the Verb, i.e. of *loving*, is Present: **amāmus** has one of the forms of Stem + Ending known as the Present **Tense** (not Future Tense—*will love*, or any other Tense).

(4) *We* (the Person of the Verb) *are affecting* someone or something by our action, by our *loving*: **amamus** is in what is called the Active **Voice** (not the Passive Voice which is used when a Person *is affected*, e.g. *is loved*).

(The Passive Voice is not used in this book)

Amāmus, then, is 1st Person Plural of the Present Tense, Active.

Here is the full Present Tense, Active:

Number	Person	Part of Verb	Meaning
Singular	1st	am-ō	*I love, am loving, do love.*
,,	2nd	amā-s	*you love, are loving, do love.*
,,	3rd	ama-t	*he, she, or it, loves, is loving, does love.*
Plural	1st	amā-mus	*we love, are loving, do love.*
,,	2nd	amā-tis	*you love, are loving, do love.*
,,	3rd	ama-nt	*they love, are loving, do love.*

The following points should be carefully noted:

1. The Stem **amā-** appears in every Person except the 1st singular where it has been absorbed in the ending.

2. *You* is used in this book for the 2nd Person singular instead of the old-fashioned *thou*.

3. Latin has only one form of Tense corresponding to the English *I love* or *am loving* or *do love*.

4. The form of the 3rd Person singular is exactly the same whether the person is *he* or *she* or *it*. In the same way, the 3rd Person plural is used for any persons or things.

1st Conjugation

Latin Verbs are divided into four main groups, called **Conjugations,** according to the last letter of the Verb Stem with which the Endings are conjugated (or *joined*). Verbs of the **amō** group, with Stems ending in -ā, belong to the 1st Conjugation.

Each Conjugation has six Tenses (corresponding to *I love, I shall love, I was loving,* etc.).

Summary of the four clues shown by the Verb Ending

Every Verb Ending will show one of:

  2 Numbers, Singular or Plural.

  3 Persons, 1st, 2nd or 3rd.

  6 Tenses, Present or Future or Imperfect, etc.

  2 Voices, Active or Passive.

Application of the four clues

If we meet the word **nāvigant,** we can now tell from the ending -nt that it is 3rd Person plural of the Present Tense, Active. We already know that the *general meaning* of **nāvigā-** is *sail*.

We now know the *exact meaning* of this part of the Verb, *they are sailing.*

Superat: we have found out from the ending, among other things, that this is a part of the Verb in the Active Voice, and that *he* or *she* or *it, is conquering* someone or something.

EXERCISE 1.

Verbs used : **nāvig-ō** *I sail.*   **labōr-ō** *I work.*
　　　　　　　explōr-ō *I spy out.* **aedific-ō** *I build.*
　　　　　　　super-ō *I conquer.* **ar-ō**　*I plough.*

Example : nāvigā-tis. Translation : *you* (pl.) *sail.*

Translate into English :

1. Nāvigā-mus.
2. Explōrā-s.
3. Labōrā-tis.
4. Ara-t.
5. Aedificā-mus.
6. Superā-s.
7. Labōra-nt.
8. Arā-mus.
9. Explōrā-mus.
10. Arā-tis.
11. Aedificā-s.
12. Explōra-nt.
13. Labōrā-mus.
14. Aedifica-nt.
15. Nāviga-t.
16. Superā-tis.

Quantities have been inserted in the first few exercises merely as a guide, in case they are taken orally.

EXERCISE 2.

Example : *he is ploughing.* Translation : **arat.**
(*N.B.* Hyphens should not be used in writing Latin.)

Translate into Latin :

1. He works.
2. They conquer.
3. You (s.) are ploughing.
4. He is building.
5. We conquer.
6. She is spying out.
7. You (pl.) build.
8. They sail.
9. I am working.
10. They do plough.
11. You (pl.) spy out.
12. She sails.
13. They are spying out.
14. We do work.
15. It conquers.
16. You (s.) are sailing.

EXERCISE 3.

Write down as many English words as you can think of, which are connected with the Latin Verbs used in Exercise 1.

EXERCISE 4.

In this exercise various parts of new Verbs are given, with the general meaning of the Stem in brackets.

Translate, and write down the 1st Person Singular of the Present Tense of:

1. Ambulā-s (walk).
2. Laudā-mus (praise).
3. Erra-t (wander).
4. Ambula-nt.
5. Laudā-s.
6. Errā-mus.
7. Clāmā-tis (shout).
8. Pugna-nt (fight).
9. Vocā-s (call).
10. Clāmā-mus.
11. Pugna-t.
12. Vocā-tis.

EXERCISE 5.

Translate into Latin:

1. We walk.
2. He is fighting.
3. They are shouting.
4. You (s.) call.
5. She praises.
6. You (pl.) are wandering.
7. It is walking.
8. They praise.
9. We call.
10. They wander.
11. You (pl.) are fighting.
12. He is shouting.

EXERCISE 6.

In this exercise the 1st Person Singular of the Latin Verb is given in brackets.

Translate into Latin:

1. We are standing (stō).
2. They ravage (vastō).
3. She is flying (volō).
4. You (s.) are seizing (occupō).
5. It is flying.
6. You (pl.) are ravaging.
7. I stand.
8. He seizes.
9. They enter (intrō).
10. We do help (iuvō).
11. He is dining (cēnō).
12. She blames (culpō).

13. You (s.) help.   15. You (pl.) are entering.
14. They blame.   16. We are dining.

EXERCISE 7.

Translate into English the following Verbs, and state their Person and Number:

(Example: culpās. Translation: *you blame*, 2nd Person singular.)

1. Culpāmus.   9. Vastās.
2. Cēnās.   10. Occupant.
3. Iuvant.   11. Intrat.
4. Occupātis.   12. Volāmus.
5. Stant.   13. Cēnant.
6. Vastat.   14. Iuvātis.
7. Intrāmus.   15. Stat.
8. Volant.   16. Culpō.

Conjunctions

In Latin, as in English, there are Conjunctions, which join words or sentences in various ways (*and* and *or* are English Conjunctions).

(1) Et is used where we use *and*:

> **Pugnant et superant.**
> *They are fighting and conquering.*

(2) **Et . . . et,** *both . . . and*:

> **Et labōrāmus et clāmāmus.**
> *We both work and shout.*

(3) **Aut . . . aut,** *either . . . or*:

> **Aut ambulat aut nāvigat.**
> *He either walks or sails.*

Vocabularies

In the first part of the book, the meanings of Latin words and the Latin for English words are given when they are first used. They are also to be found in the vocabularies at the end of the book.

EXERCISE 8.

(*a*) 1. Vocant et clāmant.
    2. Et amāmus et laudāmus.
    3. Aut arās aut aedificās.
    4. Clāmātis et pugnātis.
    5. Aut stat aut volat.
    6. Et nāvigant et explōrant.

(*b*) 1. He is wandering and shouting.
    2. She either praises or blames.
    3. We stand and shout.
    4. You (s.) are both working and having your dinner!
    5. They either shout or fight.
    6. You (pl.) conquer and ravage.

The Negative

Nōn, *not*, comes immediately before the word it affects:

> **Nōn cēnant.**
> *They are not having dinner.*

Other Common Conjunctions

(1) **Neque** or **nec,** *and not* (often separated in English), *nor*:
neque … neque or **nec … nec,** *neither … nor*:

> **Labōrāmus nec dēspērāmus.**
> *We work and do not despair.*

> **Neque arātis neque aedificātis.**
> *You neither plough nor build.*

(2) **Sed,** *but*:

> **Nōn laudō, sed culpō.**
> *I do not praise, but blame.*

EXERCISE 9.

1. Non ambulāmus, sed properāmus.
2. Pugnant nec dēspērant.
3. Non labōrāmus.
4. Ambulās, non properās.
5. Non nāvigō, sed natō.
6. Neque aedificant neque arant.
7. Oppugnant et vastant.
8. Non culpāmus, sed laudāmus.
9. Et labōrātis et iuvātis.
10. Aut laudās aut culpās.

properō, *I hurry*.　　　　　**natō,** *I swim*.
dēspērō, *I despair*.　　　　**oppugnō,** *I attack*.

EXERCISE 10.

1. I am not calling.
2. We are not having dinner, but working.
3. We either fly or sail.
4. You (pl.) are walking, not hurrying.
5. He is both attacking and conquering.
6. It neither walks nor flies: it swims.
7. They are shouting, but they are working.
8. You (s.) do not build, but ravage.
9. We stand and do not work.
10. She is calling; they do not enter.

Derivation Test

In this and other Derivation Tests which follow, write down as many English words as you can think of, which are connected with the Latin words, and the Latin words connected with the English words.

Examples: **nāvigō,** *navigate*; *culpable,* **culpō.**

(*a*) 1. **Errō.**　　　2. **Pugnō.**　　　3. **Laudō.**
(*b*) 1. Vocation.　　2. Devastate.　　3. Proclamation.

Chapter 2

The Noun (Introduction)

We now know that **labōrat,** by itself, can mean *he* or *she* or *it, is working*, and that we need not use a separate word in Latin for *he* or *she* or *it*.

But, unless we have already been told **who** *he* or *she* or *it* is, we do not know very much.

If we read *The queen reached Oxford at noon ; she came by road*, we know exactly who **she** is, because she has just been named. *The queen* gives a Name to the Person of the Verb *reached*.

Here is a Latin sentence where we have a Verb in the 3rd Person Singular and a Name is given to the Person :

> **Agricol-a labōrat.**
> *The farmer is working.*

Agricol-a is a **Noun,** which is another word for a Name (*Noun* comes from the Latin **nōmen,** *name*).

We now have a sentence which makes complete sense ; we know, at any rate, **who** is working.

Latin has no words for the English *the* or *a* : agricol-a may, therefore, be *the farmer* or *a farmer*, but the rest of a piece of continuous Latin will show us whether it is a particular (*the*) farmer, or just any (*a*) farmer in general.

Here are some more Latin Nouns, naming Persons or Things : they will be used in the next exercises :

puell-a, *girl.*	**incol-a,** *native.*
naut-a, *sailor.*	**fēmin-a,** *woman.*
rēgīn-a, *queen.*	**lūn-a,** *moon.*

All these Nouns belong to the same group and end in **-a.**

The hyphens have been put in to show that the Ending **-a** is joined to the Base of the Noun ; thus the Base of **puell-a** is **puell-.** The Base gives the *general meaning* of the Noun.

The Ending **-a** is used for any of these Nouns, when the Noun names the Person of the Verb, in the Singular.

EXERCISE 11.

Example: **naut-a clāmat**, *the sailor is shouting*.

1. Femin-a laborat.
2. Agricol-a arat.
3. Lun-a non errat.
4. Regin-a ambulat.
5. Incol-a pugnat.
6. Puell-a clamat.
7. Incol-a aedificat.
8. Naut-a explorat.
9. Agricol-a non clamat, sed laborat.
10. Regin-a non properat.

EXERCISE 12.

1. The sailor is fighting.
2. The girl is sailing.
3. The native is ploughing.
4. The farmer is having his dinner.
5. The queen enters.
6. The farmer is ploughing; the girl is not helping.
7. The girl is not having dinner, but working.
8. The sailor fights; the farmer ploughs.
9. Neither the woman nor the girl is working.
10. The moon does not hurry.

Two Nouns as the Persons of the Verb

If two Nouns are joined together by *et*, and these Nouns name the Person of the Verb, then the Verb will be in the Plural:

Agricola et fīlia labōrant.
The farmer and his daughter are working.

Note. There is one more important point to be noticed in the above example. *His*, *her*, *its* are not expressed in Latin, unless special emphasis is required. They should be used in translating from Latin into English, when the English naturally requires them; so too with 'my, our, your, their'.

EXERCISE 13.

1. Regina et filia intrant.
2. Nauta non errat.
3. Neque agricola neque filia laborat.
4. Incola aut arat aut aedificat.
5. Nauta et pugnat et superat.
6. Agricola et filia laborant.
7. Regina cenat.
8. Incola et nauta pugnant.
9. Et nauta et filia errant neque properant.
10. Agricola properat, filia ambulat.

fīlia, *daughter*.

EXERCISE 14.

1. The sailor and his daughter are shouting.
2. The queen does not hurry.
3. The farmer is calling: his daughter and the cow are wandering.
4. The farmer and his daughter shout.
5. The girl either sails or explores.
6. Both the woman and the girl are wandering.
7. The queen fights and does not despair.
8. Neither the native nor his daughter is hurrying.
9. The sailor is not working, but shouting.
10. The sailor and the girl are swimming.

cow, vacca.

Note on Translating

(*a*) In translating Latin into English, care should always be taken to see that the English is natural. Often in a vocabulary only one bare meaning is given, e.g. cēnō, *I dine*: yet the natural translation of puella cēnat may be *the girl is having dinner*, and not *the girl dines*. We must not be tied down to the idea that one

particular word in English will always be the right translation
for one particular word in Latin.

So **parāmus** could sometimes be *we get ready* instead of *we
prepare*; for **intrat** we can say *he comes in*; **errat** might be *he
wanders*, but if we have **vacca errat,** then *is straying* may be a
more fitting translation. The other words in the sentence will
generally help in the choice of a natural translation.

This also applies to Nouns: **incola** is suited sometimes by
native, sometimes by *inhabitant*.

(*b*) In the same way, thought and care are needed in translating English into Latin. If we wish to put into Latin *the sailor
cries out*, we should connect *cry out* with *shout*, and soon think
of **clāmat.** *I overcome*, *I defeat*, or *I win* should suggest *I conquer*, and so **superō.**

Derivation Test

1. Vaccination.   2. Feminine.   3. Lunatic.   4. Nautical.

Chapter 3

Nominative and Accusative Cases

So far, Nouns have only been used to name the Person of the Verb, or, to put it in another way, as the **Subject** of the Verb.

Agricola arat tells us *who* does the ploughing,—*the farmer*, and **agricola** is the Subject of **arat**.

When a Noun is used as the Subject of the Verb, it has a special form or **Case,** called the **Nominative** Case.

All the Nouns, as used in Chapter 2, were in the Nominative Case. This Case was formed by adding **-a** to the Base of the Noun.

Here is a sentence with **two** Cases in it:

> **Agricol-a terr-am arat.**
> *The farmer ploughs the land.*

Agricol-a, as we already know, is in the Nominative Case, being the **Subject** of **arat.**

Terr-am tells us *what* the farmer ploughs and is the **Direct Object** of the Verb, **arat:** it is in a special form, called the **Accusative** Case.

The Accusative Case (singular) of Nouns ending in **-a** is formed by adding **-am** to the Base. Thus the Accusatives of **rēgīn-a** and **naut-a** are **rēgīn-am, naut-am.**

Word Order

The usual order in Latin is: Subject, Object, Verb, e.g. **rēgīna fīliam culpat,** *the queen blames her daughter.*

Sometimes, especially for emphasis, the order is changed, e.g. **fīliam rēgīna culpat,** which would mean *it is her daughter the queen blames* (and not somebody else).

As a general rule, the Romans seem to have pictured the Subject first, then the Object, and then to have connected the two with the verb which fitted.

Example:	1st stage—Dog		Subject only
	2nd stage—Dog	Bone	Object as well as Subject
	3rd stage—Dog ? Bone		What is the connection to be?
	4th stage—Dog Bone Bites		Action is decided upon: the Verb appears

The dotted line which might come from a dog's eye to a bone in a Walt Disney film well illustrates the third stage. This idea of how the Romans did their thinking may or may not be correct, but it is useful to remember in studying the order of words in Latin.

Sometimes the Subject is not expressed separately, but is only shown by the ending of the Verb:

Villam intrāmus.
We enter the country house.

In this sentence the Subject is shown by the ending **-mus**, but as it is in the Verb, we keep to the usual order, and put the Verb at the end of the sentence.

In the following exercises, it should be remembered:
(1) that **-am** is added to the Base of the Noun, to form the Accusative Case, which is the Case for the Direct Object of the Verb;
(2) that the Verb is put at the end of the sentence.

EXERCISE 15.

Example: **puell-a cēn-am parat,** *the girl is preparing dinner.*

1. Regin-a fili-am vocat.
2. Agricol-a cas-am aedificat.
3. Silv-am intramus.
4. Naut-a stell-am non spectat.
5. Agricol-am puell-a iuvat.
6. Fili-a regin-am delectat.
7. Mens-am portas.
8. Vill-am, non cas-am aedificamus.

  9. Agricol-a et fili-a vacc-am spectant.
 10. Vacc-a errat et cas-am intrat.

casa, *cottage.*	**dēlectō,** *I delight, please.*
silva, *wood.*	**mensa,** *table.*
stella, *star.*	**portō,** *I carry.*
spectō, *I watch, look at.*[1]	**villa,** *country-house, farm.*

[1] No separate Latin word is needed to translate *at*: it is already contained in **spectō** (compare **exspectō,** *I wait for*).

EXERCISE 16.

  1. The sailor is looking at the little boat.
  2. The farmer is going into the cottage.
  3. The little boat delights the girl.
  4. The sailor and the girl are helping the farmer.
  5. You (pl.) are entering the wood.
  6. His dinner pleases the farmer.
  7. The farmer and his daughter are ploughing the land.
  8. You (s.) are helping the sailor.
  9. The queen and her daughter are entering the little boat.
 10. The farmer is calling the cow.

little boat, **nāvicula.**   *dinner,* **cēna.**   *land,* **terra.**

Transitive and Intransitive Verbs

Verbs such as **occupō,** *I seize,* and **culpō,** *I blame,* which have their Direct Object in the Accusative Case, are called **Transitive** Verbs. Such Verbs must affect some person or thing, to complete their sense. We at once ask *I seize **what?** I blame **whom?***

Verbs which do not have a Direct Object, but which already have a complete meaning in themselves, are called **Intransitive** Verbs.

Experience will show which Latin Verbs are Intransitive Verbs. It is most important that they should never be used with a Direct Object.

The following Verbs, which have already been used in this book, are all Intransitive, i.e. they cannot take an Accusative Case:

ambulō, *I walk.*	**pugnō,** *I fight.*
nāvigō, *I sail.*	**volō,** *I fly.*
errō, *I wander.*	**stō,** *I stand.*
clāmō, *I shout.*	**cēnō,** *I dine.*
labōrō, *I work.*	**natō,** *I swim.*

In English we can say *he fought the dragon*, but in Latin
pugnō cannot govern a Direct Object and a word would be used
to join *fought* and *dragon*, called a Preposition, e.g. **contrā,**
against. Prepositions will be dealt with later.

Many Latin Transitive Verbs, on the other hand, are used by
themselves, without an Object being expressed, because we can
easily in our minds supply an Object:

> **Agricola aedificat,** *the farmer is building* (*a house, shed, etc.*).
> **Incola superat,** *the native is conquering* (*his enemy*), or, as
> we would more likely say, *is winning*.

EXERCISE 17.

1. Nauta insulam occupat.
2. Fortuna agricolam iuvat.
3. Puella mensam portat et cenam parat.
4. Incola viam monstrat.
5. Regina villam intrat.
6. Nauta oram spectat.
7. Pecuniam non postulamus.
8. Puella epistolam exspectat.
9. Agricola non aedificat, sed terram arat.
10. Nauta et filia insulam spectant.

insula, *island.*	**ōra,** *shore.*
fortūna, *fortune.*	**pecūnia,** *money.*
parō, *I prepare.*	**postulō,** *I demand.*
via, *way, road.*	**epistola,** *letter.*
monstrō, *I show.*	**exspectō,** *I wait for, expect.*

EXERCISE 18.

1. We are expecting a letter.
2. The girl is demanding money.

3. The letter pleases the queen.
4. The queen does not blame the sailor.
5. The wood hides the road.
6. Fortune does not help the sailor.
7. The cow demands water.
8. Neither moon nor star shows the way.
9. The water delights the cow.
10. The girl does not hide, but shows, the letter.

I hide, **cēlō**.   *water*, **aqua**.

EXERCISE 19.

BEFORE THE ROMANS CAME

A British farmer settles down in what is now Shropshire, in, say, 100 B.C.

Agricola primo silvam explorat et viam secat; deinde terram parat et casam aedificat. Fortuna agricolam iuvat; Sabrina aquam, silva umbram suppeditat. Tandem agricola et filia casam habitant; vaccam curant, terram arant, herbam secant. Interdum agricola plagam parat et feram necat; ita cenam suppeditat. Filia agricolam exspectat; agricola non errat, quod luna viam monstrat; casam tandem intrat. Filia agricolam salutat et cenam parat; cena et agricolam et filiam delectat.

Words:

prīmō, *at first*.	**herba**, *grass*.
secō, *I cut*.	**interdum**, *sometimes*.
deīnde, *next, then*.	**plaga**, *net, trap*.
Sabrīna, the river *Severn*.	**fera**, *wild beast*.
umbra, *shade*.	**necō**, *I kill*.
suppeditō, *I provide, supply*.	**ita**, *in this way, so*.
tandem, *at last*.	**quod**, *because*.
habitō, *I inhabit, live in*.	**salūtō**, *I greet*.
cūrō, *I look after*.	

EXERCISE 20.

The girl cuts the hay and carries water; then she calls and looks after the cow. She waits for the farmer for a long time.

At last the farmer enters the cottage; he cries out and greets his daughter. He is carrying his net and a wild beast. His daughter greets the farmer and gets ready the supper.

Words:

hay, use **herba.**   *supper,* **cēna.**

for a long time, **diū.**

Derivation Test

(*a*) 1. **Spectō.**   2. **Terra.**   3. **Habitō.**   4. **Salūtō.**

     5. **Insula.**   6. **Portō.**   7. **Fortūna.**   8. **Monstrō.**

(*b*) 1. Curate.   2. Stellar.   3. Umbrella.   4. Expect.

     5. Aquatic.   6. Herbaceous.   7. Epistle.   8. Impecunious.

Chapter 4
Vocative Case

Cēn-am, ō fīli-a, parāmus.

It is not difficult to see what this sentence means: *we are getting dinner ready, my daughter*. The person making the statement is addressing his daughter.

Fīli-a is in the **Vocative** Case (from **vocō,** *I call*), which is used for directly addressing a person, place, or thing; **ō** can be put in before the Vocative, or left out; it should be put in, if it makes the sense more clear, for in the singular the Vocative of a Noun ending in **-a** has the same form as the Nominative.

Iūlia, rēgīna, appropinquat, could mean either *Julia, O queen, is approaching* or *Julia, the queen, is approaching*, but if we put **ō** before **rēgīna,** then **rēgīna** can only be Vocative.

EXERCISE 21.

Turn to Exercise 13, and put in a Vocative Case in each sentence, i.e. let the sentences be addressed to someone. Remember to put in **ō**, if it makes the sense more clear.

1st Conjugation: Imperative Active

All the parts of Verbs so far used have made statements about facts, e.g. **cēnam parāmus.**

These Verb-forms all belong to what is called the **Indicative Mood.**

To express a Command, we use another group of Verb-forms, called the **Imperative Mood (imperō,** *I command*):

The 2nd pers. sing. of the Imperative, Active, of **amō** is **amā,**
love.

The 2nd pers. plur. of the Imperative, Active, of **amō** is **amāte,**
love.

This Mood of the Verb is naturally often found after or before a Vocative Case:

Cornēlia, villam intrā.
Cornelia, go into the house.

Villam intrāte, Cornēlia et Clōdia.
Go into the house, Cornelia and Clodia.

EXERCISE 22.

(a) 1. Ara terram, agricola.
2. Villam aedificate.
3. Lunam specta, o filia.
4. O Minerva et Diana, puellam conservate.
5. Vaccam vita, Clodia.

      conservō, *I keep safe.*   **vītō,** *I avoid.*

(b) 1. Cut the grass, farmer.
2. Get the anchor ready, sailor.
3. Hurry up, Clodia and Cornelia.
4. Call the maid, my[1] daughter.
5. Hide (pl.) the money.

   anchor, **ancora.**   *maid, maid-servant,* **ancilla.**

[1] See note on p. 26

Chapter 5

1st Declension: Nominative, Vocative, and Accusative Cases, Singular and Plural

The group of Nouns which have their Nom. sing. ending in **-a** is called the 1st **Declension.** There are five Declensions in all.

The original idea seems to have been that the Nominative Case was the upright Case and the others fell away from it, or *declined*, thus:

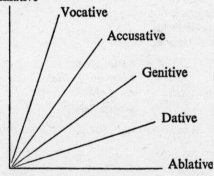

All the Cases, except the Nom. and Voc., are known as the Oblique (*slanting*) Cases.

(We shall come to the last three Cases later.)

When we are asked to decline a Noun, we repeat the Cases in the order shown above.

Nouns, like Verbs, have 2 Numbers, Singular and Plural.

Here is the plan of the first three Cases of the 1st Declension both Singular and Plural:

Singular.

Case		Meaning	Use
Nominative	**mensa**	*table*	as Subject
Vocative	**mensa**	*O table*	for addressing a table
Accusative	**mensam**	*table*	as Direct Object

Plural.

Case		Meaning	Use
Nominative	**mensae**	*tables*	as Subject
Vocative	**mensae**	*O tables*	for addressing tables
Accusative	**mensās**	*tables*	as Direct Object

EXERCISE 23.

1. Puellae cenam exspectant.
2. Fortuna nautas iuvat.
3. Sagittas parate.
4. Agricola vaccas vocat.
5. Nautae victoriam non reportant.
6. Copiae hastas comparant.
7. Silvae dant umbram.
8. Incolas oppugnate, o nautae.
9. Praeda nautas delectat.
10. Epistolas exspectamus.

sagitta, *arrow*.	**hasta**, *spear*.
victōria, *victory*.	**comparō**, *I obtain*.
reportō, *I win* (*bring back*).	**dō**, *I give*.
cōpiae (pl.), *troops*.	**praeda**, *booty*.

cōpia in the sing. means *plenty*; in the plur. *troops, forces*.

EXERCISE 24.

FIRST ROMAN EXPEDITION TO BRITAIN

Julius Caesar leads an expedition to Britain (55 B.C.). *Caesar thought that so long as Britain was not occupied by Rome, it would threaten the peace of Gaul. His invasion, however, did not lead to occupation.*

Caesar et copiae appropinquant et oram explorant.[1] Incolae copias spectant; et sagittas et essedas statim parant. Primum advenas propulsant; deinde advenae hastas iactant,

[1] Caesar found it impossible to land at Dover (**Dubrae**), where British tribesmen were waiting for him on the steep cliffs, so he landed on a flat beach near Deal.

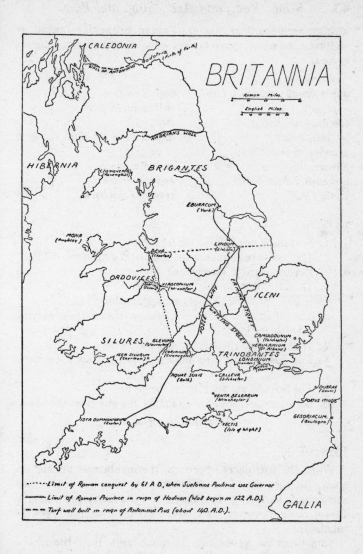

CALEDONIA

WALL OF ANTONINUS • Bodotria (Firth of Forth)

BRITANNIA

Roman Miles.

English Miles.

HADRIAN'S WALL

HIBERNIA

BRIGANTES

Cianoventa
(Rovenglass)

EBURACUM
(York.)

MONA
(Anglesey)

DEVA
(Chester)

LINDUM
(Lincoln.)

ORDOVICES

VIROCONIUM
(Wroxeter)

ICENI

FOSSE WAY

WATLING STREET

ERMINE STREET

SILURES

GLEVUM
(Gloucester)

CAMULODUNUM
(Colchester)

VERULAMIUM
(St Albans)

ISCA SILURUM
(Caerleon)

CORINIUM
(Cirencester)

TRINOBANTES

LONDINIUM
(London)

AQUAE SULIS
(Bath)

CALLEVA
(Silchester)

DUBRAE
(Dover)

VENTA BELGARUM
(Winchester)

PORTUS ITIUS

ISCA DUMNONIORUM
(Exeter)

VECTIS
(Isle of Wight)

GESORIACUM
(Boulogne)

GALLIA

‑‑‑‑‑‑‑ Limit of Roman conquest by 61 A.D, when Suetonius Paulinus was Governor

⎯⎯⎯⎯ Limit of Roman Province in reign of Hadrian (Wall begun in 122 A.D).

▬ ▬ ▬ Turf wall built in reign of Antoninus Pius (about 140 A.D).

incolas oppugnant et fugant. Caesar Britanniam vastat et victoriam reportat; mox tamen, quod procella instat, copias revocat.

Words:

appropinquō (intrans.), *I approach.*
esseda, *war-chariot.*
statim, *at once.*
prīmum, *at first.*
advena, *foreigner.*
prōpulsō, *I drive back.*
iactō, *I hurl.*

fugō, *I rout.*
Britannia, *Britain.*
mox, *soon.*
tamen, *however* (2nd word in
  clause).
procella, *storm.*
instō, *I threaten.*
revocō, *I call back.*

EXERCISE 25.

1. Fortune is not helping the foreigners.
2. The cows are coming near, because the farmer is calling.
3. Reconnoitre (pl.) the woods.
4. The letter does not please the girls.
5. Hurry! (pl.) The chariots are approaching.
6. The inhabitants are awake, because the troops are laying waste the land.
7. Farmers, you are keeping safe the country.
8. The inhabitants are building cottages, not country-houses.
9. The farmers are waiting for the moon.
10. Because the troops are attacking, the girl hides the cows.

I am awake, **vigilō.**

EXERCISE 26.

When the foreigners approach, the inhabitants do not despair. Because they love their country, they get ready their spears and chariots. At first they throw the foreigners into confusion. Soon, however, the troops enter the island and rout the inhabitants.

Sometimes the woods hide the inhabitants; then[1] the inhabitants prepare an ambush and attack the troops. Caesar at length wins a victory, but he does not conquer the island.

Words:

when, **ubi.**	*ambush,* **insidiae** (pl.).
country, **patria.**	*but . . . not,* **nec tamen.**
I throw into confusion, **perturbō.**	

Note. **Patria,** *country,* in the sense of *native land.*

Terra, *a country,* or *earth, land.*

[1] *Then* (*at that time*), **tum;** *then* (*next,* in order of events), **tum** or **deīnde.**

Additional exercises on the Accusative of Direct Object:

EXERCISE 27.

1. Agricola filias amat.
2. Aqua vitam suppeditat.
3. Agricola pecuniam conservat.
4. Hasta nautam vulnerat.
5. Puella gallinas curat.
6. Aquam ancilla portat.
7. Incolae nautas fugant.
8. Italiam advenae spectant.
9. Nauta naviculam gubernat.
10. Copiae portam intrant.

vīta, *life.*	**Ītalia,** *Italy.*
vulnerō, *I wound.*	**gubernō,** *I steer.*
gallīna, *hen.*	**porta,** *gate* (*of a city*).

EXERCISE 28.

1. The farmers are hiding their[1] cows.
2. The sailor saves his country.
3. The queen demands troops.
4. We are freeing our[1] country, my daughter.
5. The troops attack the island.
6. The sailor is showing the way.
7. The foreigners are entering the island.
8. The maid is going into the cottage.
9. It is his daughter that the farmer is calling. (*N.B.* Latin order.)

[1] See note on p. 26

10. Hens love water.

I free, **līberō.**

EXERCISE 29.

1. Copiae fossam explorant.
2. Nautae pugnam parant.
3. Agricola vaccam liberat.
4. Aquam conservate, nautae.
5. Regina copias excitat.
6. Nautae victoriam reportant.
7. Copiae hastas iactant.
8. Regina copias non culpat.
9. Advenae vias et silvas explorant.
10. Oram nautae spectant.

fossa, *ditch.*   **pugna,** *fight, battle.*   **excitō,** *I rouse.*

EXERCISE 30.

1. The troops are attacking the island.
2. The queen watches the troops.
3. The natives worship a goddess.
4. We are examining the shore.
5. The cows do not attack the farmer nor his daughter.
6. The troops are expecting a victory.
7. The earth supplies plenty.
8. The cow comes near and goes into the ditch.
9. Either work (s.) or go into the house!
10. The girl is hiding her letter.

I worship, **adōrō.**   *goddess*, **dea.**

Questions

There are several ways of introducing a question in Latin:

(1) **-ne** is used for a simple question which asks for information; it is attached to the end of the first word in the sentence, which should be the important word in the question:

Filiamne exspectās?
*Are you waiting for your daughter? (Is it your daughter
you are waiting for?)*

(2) **nonne** is used to introduce a question which contains the
negative and of which the expected answer is *yes*:

Nonne epistolam exspectās?
*Aren't you expecting a letter? (i.e. Surely you do
expect a letter?)*

(3) **num** is used to introduce a question, when an answer is not
expected and is already felt to be *no*:

Num amīcitiam vītās?
Surely you don't avoid friendship?

(4) There are many other words used to introduce a question:

ubi? *where?*	**quō?** *whither, to where?*
unde? *whence, from where?*	**quot?** *how many?*
cūr? *why?*	**cūr ... nōn?** *why ... not?*

EXERCISE 31.

1. Epistolamne agricola exspectat?
2. Num desperamus?
3. Nonne praeda nautas delectat?
4. Ubi copiae hiemant?
5. Quot villas aedificant?
6. Cur terram vastatis?
7. Nonne fabulae puellas delectant?
8. Num lunam habitas?
9. Vigilantne copiae?
10. Quo properas, o puella?

hiemō, *I spend the winter.*   **fābula,** *story.*

EXERCISE 32

1. Where are you (s.) hiding the money?
2. From where is he recalling his forces?
3. Are the girls looking at the cow?

4. Where are the troops hurrying to?
5. Does not the moon show the way?
6. Surely you don't blame the cow, farmer?
7. Why do the forces not conquer Britain?
8. Do the troops dread the chariots?
9. Why are you (pl.) examining the woods?
10. Is it the queen they are waiting for?

I dread, **reformīdō.**

Derivation Test

(*a*) 1. **Victōria.** 2. **Conservō.** 3. **Fābula.** 4. **Dēspērō.**

(*b*) 1. Patriotic. 2. Copious. 3. Revoke. 4. Vigilant.

Chapter 6
Genitive Case

(1) **Agricol-ae fīli-a vill-am intrat.**
   The daughter of the farmer is entering the house.

(2) **Turb-am naut-ārum spectāmus.**
   We are watching a crowd of sailors.

Agricol-ae, *of the farmer*, and **naut-ārum**, *of sailors*, are in the Case called the **Genitive**.

This Case has many uses, but almost always it can be translated by *of* in English (though in the above example a more natural translation would be *the farmer's daughter*).

The Genitive may come after or before the Noun with which it is connected, e.g. **fīlia agricolae** or **agricolae fīlia**.

The Genitive Sing. of the 1st Decl. ends in -ae;
the Genitive Plur. of the 1st Decl. ends in -ārum.

EXERCISE 33.
1. Copiae vaccas agricolae postulant.
2. Victoriamne incolarum nuntias?
3. Vacca ianuam villae spectat, nec tamen intrat.
4. Copiae oram insulae tandem explorant.
5. Umbram silvae non vitamus.
6. Incolarum essedas reformidamus.
7. Non patriae oram spectatis.
8. Feminae ianuam tabernae intrant.
9. Quot vaccas filia agricolae curat?
10. Nonne filiae villam amas?

nuntiō, *I announce.* **iānua,** *door.* **taberna,** *shop.*
45

EXERCISE 34.

ROMAN OCCUPATION OF BRITAIN

The Romans invade Britain (A.D. 43) *and make it into a province of the Roman Empire. Claudius was Emperor and the expedition was led by Aulus Plautius.*

Rursus advenae incolas Britanniae oppugnant victoriamque[1] saepe reportant; et Druidas[2] et copias reginae Boudiccae[3] superant; Britanniam tamen non omnino superant. Colonias collocant, balneas, villas, tabernas aedificant.

Incolae Britanniae terram arant et laborant; copiae vaccas agricolarum et pecuniam saepe postulant; avaritia copiarum iram incolarum excitat; interdum tamen amicitia advenarum incolas delectat.

Words:

rursus, *again.*	collocō, *I establish.*
saepe, *often.*	balneae (pl.), *baths.*
Druidae, *Druids.*	avāritia, *greed.*
omnīnō, *altogether.*	īra, *anger.*
colōnia, *colony, settlement.*	amīcitia, *friendship.*

[1] -que, attached to the end of a word, is often used instead of et, *and*, before a word.

[2] Druidas. The Druids are described by Caesar as acting as priests, judges, and schoolmasters.

[3] Boudiccae. Boudicca (generally, though wrongly, called Boadicea) was queen of the Icēni who lived in Norfolk, Suffolk and Cambridgeshire. She led a serious revolt against the Romans in A.D. 61.

EXERCISE 35.

1. A crowd of women is looking at the shop.
2. Call (s.) the farmer's cows.
3. The maids are rousing the anger of their mistress.
4. Are you (s.) getting ready the sailor's little boat?
5. The natives' victory does not please the troops.
6. Boadicea lays waste the settlements of the foreigners.
7. The memory of wrongs rouses the inhabitants.
8. Look (pl.) at the shore of your native land.

9. The inhabitants of Scotland do not dread the troops.
10. Why is the farmer's daughter not working?

crowd, **turba**.   *wrong*, **iniūria**.
mistress (*of household*), **domina**.   *Scotland*, **Calēdonia**.
memory, **memoria**.

EXERCISE 36.

The troops of the foreigners again approach and enter
Britain. The nature of the land often helps the natives; at
length, however, the troops almost conquer the island. The
foreigners build country-houses and establish colonies, but they
are always demanding the cows and money of the natives and
are obtaining booty. The wrongdoings of the foreigners rouse
the anger of Boadicea. Boadicea does not despair, but calls
together her troops. The troops of Boadicea soon lay waste the
colonies.

Words:
nature, **nātūra**.   *always*, **semper**.
almost, **paene**.   *I call together*, **convocō**.

Additional Exercises on the Genitive Case:

EXERCISE 37.

1. Tabernae incolarum copias non delectant.
2. Agricolae vacca errat.
3. Copiae Boudiccae colonias cremant.
4. Turba incolarum villas intrat.
5. Vaccae umbram silvae amant.
6. Epistola filiae nautam delectat.
7. Agricolae vaccas vitate.
8. Cur fortunam patriae culpatis?
9. Incolae statuam deae adorant.
10. Fabulae ancillae dominam fatigant.

cremō, *I burn*.   **statua**, *statue*.   **fatīgō**, *I tire* (trans.).

Exercise 38.

1. Troops do not enter the gates of Rome.
2. The sailor is getting the girls' boat ready.
3. The inhabitants of the island drive back the foreigners.
4. The foreigners are demanding the farmers' cows.
5. There stands the altar of the goddess.
6. The natives' victory pleases Boadicea.
7. The Severn supplies plenty of water.
8. Don't you like the queen's statue?
9. The foreigners' shops delight the farmers' daughters.
10. Look (pl.) again at the shore of France.

Rome, **Rōma.** *altar*, **āra.**
there, **ibi.** *France*, **Gallia.**

Derivation Test

(*a*) 1. **Porta.**   2. **Iniūria.**   3. **Fatīgō**
     4. **Nātūra.**   5. **Iānua.**   6. **Līberō.**

(*b*) 1. Colonial.   2. Tavern.   3. Adorable.
     4. Report.   5. Memorial.   6. Avarice.

Chapter 7
Dative Case

(1) **Agricol-a aqu-am vacc-ae dat.**
The farmer is giving water to the cow.

Vacc-ae, *to the cow*, is in the Case called the **Dative** (a word which comes from the Verb **dō**, *I give*, and so describes the *giving* Case). This Case is used to express *to* after Verbs of *giving, showing, telling* and *promising*, but is not used to express motion *to* a place.

The Dative Plur. of the 1st Declension ends in -**īs**, e.g. **vacc-īs,** *to the cows*.

So : **Incola viam cōpiīs monstrat.**
The inhabitant shows the way to the troops.

Fābulās advenīs narrāmus.
We tell stories to the strangers.

In the above examples **aquam, viam, fābulās** are Direct Objects of the Verbs; **vaccae, cōpiīs, advenīs** are **Indirect Objects** of the Verbs.

N.B. In English we often put the Indirect Object first and leave out the word *to*, e.g. *the farmer is giving the cow water*. In translating into Latin we must carefully consider the meaning of the English and distinguish between the Direct Object and the Indirect Object.

(2) **Agricol-a vill-am fīli-ae aedificat.**
The farmer is building a house for his daughter, or *his daughter a house.*

In this use the Dative expresses *for whom* someone does something, and is often called the Dative of **Advantage**: the farmer builds a house for the advantage of his daughter.

Sometimes we find a Dative of Disadvantage :

Insidiās incolīs parāmus.
We prepare an ambush for the inhabitants.

The Dative Sing. of the 1st Decl. ends in **-ae;**
the Dative Plur. of the 1st Decl. ends in **-īs.**

The sense of a sentence will help in showing whether a form
ending in **-ae** is Genitive or Dative Sing., or Nominative or
Vocative Plur.

EXERCISE 39.

1. Puella vaccas copiis non monstrat.
2. Num victoriam incolis nuntias?
3. Luna nautae viam monstrat.
4. Ancilla cenam dominae parat.
5. Pecuniam et vaccas advenis saepe damus.
6. Interdum copiae amicitiam incolis praestant.
7. Da gallinis aquam.
8. Pugnam advenis parate.
9. Aqua dat nautis vitam.
10. Advenae villas balneasque incolis insulae ostentant.

praestō, *I offer, give.* **ostentō,** *I display.*

EXERCISE 40.

CONQUEST OF ANGLESEY

*Suētōnius Paulīnus, governor of Britain, attacks the island of
Mona (Anglesey),* A.D. 61.

Druidae et perfugae Monam habitant. Suetonius hastas et
galeas copiis suppeditat et oram insulae monstrat; naviculas
parat copiasque transportat. Druidae feminis praestant taedas;
incolae enim Britanniae etiam feminis pugnas mandant.
Feminae taedas iactant, copias perturbant. Suetonius tamen
copias incitat. Fortuna tandem copiis dat victoriam. Suetonius
victoriam copiarum incolis Romae nuntiat.

Words:
perfuga, *fugitive.* **enim,** *for* (always 2nd word in clause).
galea, *helmet.* **etiam,** *even, also.*

transportō, *I carry across.*
taeda, *torch.*

mandō, *I entrust.*
incitō, *I rouse, encourage.*

Exercise 41.

1. The farmer is pointing out the moon to his daughter.
2. The inhabitants entrust the fight to Boadicea.
3. The wood gives the cows shade.
4. Do not the settlements supply booty to the natives of Britain?
5. Get ready (pl.) the little boats for the troops.
6. Fortune often gives plenty to the farmers.
7. I am pointing out to the girl the coast of France.
8. The natives announce a victory to the queen.
9. Boadicea does not give pardon to the foreigners.
10. The natives display their chariots to the queen.

pardon, **venia.**

Exercise 42.

Suetonius carries his troops across. The Druids point out the little boats to the inhabitants of the island and give torches to the women. The women dread neither troops nor spears; they shout and hurl their torches. Soon, however, the troops throw the Druids and women into confusion. Perhaps because they entrust the battle to women, the Druids do not win a victory.

Word: *perhaps*, **fortasse.**

Additional exercises on the Dative:

Exercise 43.

1. Veniam da filiae.
2. Sabrina aquam incolis suppeditat.
3. Fabulamne filiae narras?
4. Incolae pecuniam advenis non ostentant.
5. Aram Fortunae consecramus.
6. Nonne agricola herbam vaccis parat?

7. Ancilla agricolae cenam portat.
8. Suppeditate hastas copiis.
9. Agricola filiae dat vaccam.
10. Insidias advenis parate.

　　narrō, *I tell, recount.*　　**consecrō,** *I dedicate.*

EXERCISE 44.

1. The farmer is preparing a trap for the wild animal.
2. The moon shows the troops the ambush.
3. The Druids are dedicating an altar to Minerva.
4. The farmer entrusts his cows to the girl.
5. Show (s.) the way to the stranger.
6. I tell my daughter stories.
7. The inhabitants often offer friendship to foreigners.
8. A letter announces his daughter's victory to the farmer.
9. The sailor is building a little boat for his daughter.
10. We entrust our lives to the sailors.

Derivation Test

1. Vital.　2. Narrative.　3. Ostentatious.　4. Consecration.

Chapter 8

Ablative Case

This Case has four main uses. We will deal with two of them first.

(1) **Fēmin-a taed-am dextr-ā iactat.**
   The woman is throwing a torch with her right hand.

   Cōpi-ae hast-īs pugnant.
   The troops are fighting with spears.

Dextrā, *with her right hand,* and **hastīs,** *with spears,* are both in the Case called the **Ablative.** It is used here to express something *with* which you do something. In the examples above **dextrā** and **hastīs** are known as Ablatives of Instrument: *spears* are the *instruments* with which the troops fight.

(2) **Incol-ae cum Boudicc-ā properant.**
   The inhabitants are hurrying with Boadicea.

In this example the Ablative is used with the **Preposition cum** to express *in company with.* The Ablative is never used in this way without the help of **cum.** This Ablative is called the Ablative of Accompaniment.

These two Ablatives, of Instrument and Accompaniment, must be carefully distinguished. In English we use *with* for both of them, and, in translating English into Latin, we must consider which kind of Ablative is needed, i.e. Ablative alone or Ablative with **cum.**

The Ablative Sing. of the 1st Decl. ends in -**ā**;
the Ablative Plur. of the 1st Decl. ends in -**īs.**

Now that we know something about all the Cases, it is time to set out the full Declension, Singular and Plural, of a 1st Declension Noun. Some of the uses of the Cases are already known; there are other uses which will be explained in this chapter and in Chapter 9 (a complete plan, with meanings and uses of Cases is given at the beginning of Chapter 10).

mensa, *table.*

Base   mens-

Case	Singular	Plural
Nominative	mensa	mensae
Vocative	mensa	mensae
Accusative	mensam	mensās
Genitive	mensae	mensārum
Dative	mensae	mensīs
Ablative	mensā	mensīs

EXERCISE 45.

1. Nauta filiam fabulis delectat.
2. Copias sagittis fugamus.
3. Domina cum ancilla laborat.
4. Nauta puellam navicula delectat.
5. Caesar cum copiis appropinquat.
6. Praedam pugna[1] comparamus.
7. Agricola viam dextra monstrat.
8. Silvam cum filia exploro.
9. Incolas amicitia conciliate.
10. Interdum copiae villas flamma vastant.

dextra, *right hand.* **conciliō,** *I win over.* **flamma,** *flame.*

[1] *By* is sometimes the right English Preposition, not *with*.

EXERCISE 46.

1. The women rout the troops with their torches.
2. Point out (s.) the coast with your right hand.
3. Even the women fight with the Druids.
4. Work (pl.) with the farmer.
5. We do not obtain friendship by battle.
6. Boadicea hurries with her troops.
7. The farmer pleases the cows with hay and water.

8. The troops ravage the colonies with flames.
9. We win over the inhabitants by friendship.
10. The farmer is having supper with his daughter.

Ablative Case (continued)

(3) **Ā Britanni-ā nāvigāmus.**
We sail from Britain.

Here the Ablative is used with a Preposition to express *from*; **ā** is generally used before a consonant, **ab** always before a vowel or *h*, e.g. **ab Ītaliā,** *from Italy.*

So too, **ex** or **ē** (ex always before a vowel), *out of, from,* is used with the Ablative:

> **Ē silv-ā properat.**
> *He hurries out of the wood.*

> **Cōpi-ās ex insul-ā revocat.**
> *He recalls the troops out of the island.*

(4) **Incol-ae vacc-ās in silv-īs cēlant.**
The natives hide their cows in the woods.

> **Puell-a in aqu-ā fluitat.**
> *The girl is floating on the water.*

In these examples the Ablative is used with the Preposition **in** to express *in* and *on.*

EXERCISE 47.

1. Copiae ab Italia properant.
2. Epistolam a filia exspectamus.
3. Druidae in ora pugnant.
4. Aquamne in galea portas?
5. Incolae copias ex ora propulsant.
6. Vaccae a via errant.
7. Caesar copias ex Gallia transportat.
8. Incolas a catenis liberate.
9. In silva cum filia ambulo.
10. Cur nauta stat in navicula?

catēna, *chain.*

EXERCISE 48.

1. Boadicea is standing in her chariot.
2. The farmer frees the cow from its chain.
3. The foreigners soon establish colonies in Britain.
4. A statue of the goddess stands on the gate.
5. The girl obtains water out of the Severn.
6. In the wood there stands an altar.
7. The troops are routing the natives in the battle.
8. We are expecting a victory from the troops.
9. Where is the farmer hurrying to out of the cottage?
10. The cows are wandering on the shore.

Exercises on the four main uses of the Ablative:

EXERCISE 49.

1. Suetonius copias naviculis transportat.
2. Druidae cum feminis in ora stant.
3. Copiae ab ora insulae appropinquant.
4. Cur pecuniam in terra celas?
5. Feminae ex turba Druidarum taedas iactant.
6. Druidae feminas taedis armant.
7. Amicitiam benevolentia confirmamus.
8. Fossane villam circumdas?
9. Incolae cum Boudicca copias fugant.
10. Cur copiae in colonia hiemant?

armō, *I arm.*   confirmō, *I strengthen.*
benevolentia, *kindness.*   circumdō, *I surround.*

EXERCISE 50.

DETECTION OF THE ROBBER CĀCUS

The hero Hercules was doomed to obey the command of Eurystheus, king of Mycēnae, a city in Greece. One of his twelve labours was to kill a three-headed monster at Gādes (Cadiz), called Gēryōn, and bring back his herds. On the way back Hercules takes a rest near the river Tiber in Italy.

Hercules in Italia cum vaccis errat. Forte, dum vaccae aquam potant, dormitat. Ibi tamen Cacus in spelunca habitat :[1] vaccas spectat et e spelunca clam properat; aliquot vaccas separat et praedam in spelunca celat. Et Cacus et vaccae speluncam retro intrant; ita ungulae vaccarum latebras non indicant. Mane tamen spelunca resonat, quod vaccae clamant. Hercules incolam speluncae clava oppugnat vaccasque reciperat. Vaccam ibi immolat et aram consecrat.

Words:

forte, *by chance.*	**ungula,** *hoof.*
dum, *while.*	**latebrae** (pl.), *hiding-place.*
pōtō, *I drink.*	**indicō,** *I show, betray.*
dormītō, *I fall asleep.*	**māne,** *in the morning.*
spēlunca, *cave.*	**resonō,** *I echo.*
clam, *secretly.*	**clāva,** *club.*
aliquot, *some.*	**reciperō,** *I recover.*
sēparō, *I separate.*	**immolō,** *I sacrifice.*
retrō, *backwards.*	

[1] **habitō** is sometimes used transitively with an Acc. (*I inhabit*) but more often intransitively (*I live, dwell*) with **in** and Abl.

EXERCISE 51.

1. The sailor is pointing out the island with his right hand.
2. The eagles are flying from the wood.
3. Even the queen fights with the forces of the natives.
4. Why does the maid tire the mistress with her stories?
5. The natives fly out from their ambush.
6. The girls are swimming in the water.
7. Out of the house walks a cow!
8. The farmers are surrounding the wild animal with nets.
9. Strengthen (pl.) friendship by kindness.
10. The queen is arming the inhabitants with spears and helmets.

eagle, **aquila.**   *I fly out,* **ēvolō.**

EXERCISE 52.

Cacus lives in a cave. He plunders the country and devours even the inhabitants, if they come near. When Hercules approaches with his cows, Cacus without delay hurries out of the cave and looks at the cows. He hopes for a dinner and hides some cows in the cave. Hercules, however, recognises his cows in the morning, because they cry out. He hurries from the road and takes the cave by storm. Then he overcomes the inhabitant of the cave with his club and hastens with his cows from Italy.

Words:

I devour, **dēvorō**.	*I hope for*, **spērō**.
if, **sī**.	*I recognise*, **noscitō**.
without, **sine** (with Abl.).	*I take by storm*, **expugnō**.
delay, **mora**.	

Derivation Test

(*a*) 1. **Confirmō** 2. **Flamma**.   3. **Conciliō**. 4. **Benevolentia**.

(*b*) 1. **Indicator**. 2. **Recuperate**. 3. **Aquiline**. 4. **Resonant**.

Chapter 9

Prepositions with Accusative Case

Herculēs ad spēluncam properat.
Hercules hurries to the cave.

Nautae ad ōram appropinquant.
The sailors come near to (approach) the shore.

Puella in silvam errat.
The girl wanders into the wood.

Ad, *to* or *towards*, **in**, *into* (sometimes *against*), are both Prepositions which take the Accusative.

It should be particularly noticed that **appropinquō**, *I approach*, is intransitive and is followed by **ad**.

In, *into*, must be carefully distinguished from **in**, *in*, or *on*, which takes the Ablative.

Other common Prepositions which take the Accusative are:

ante, *before, in front of*.	**post**, *after, behind*.
contrā, *against*.	**praeter**, *along, except*.
ob, **propter**, *on account of, because of*.	**prope**, *near*.
per, *through, throughout, by means of*.	**trans**, *across*.

EXERCISE 53.

1. Boudicca et copiae ad coloniam properant.
2. Puellae ante cenam saepe natant.
3. Villam prope silvam aedificamus.
4. Num post victoriam desperatis?
5. Taedisne feminae contra copias pugnant?
6. Nautae propter procellam non navigant.
7. Trans Hadriam navigamus.
8. Copias in coloniam revoca.
9. Feminae per vias ambulant.

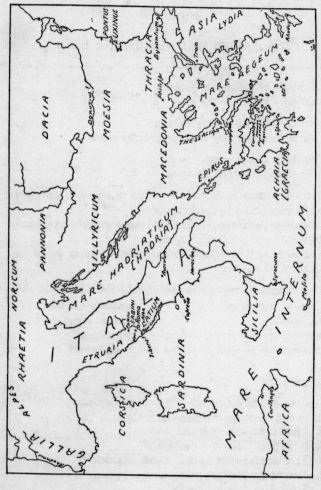

Map showing the places in Italy and the eastern Mediterranean area which occur in this book.

10. Ancillae ad¹ agricolae villam appropinquant.

Hadria. *Adriatic Sea.*

¹ **ad** must be taken with **villam:** just as in English we say *I am going to Mr. Jones's house,* where *Mr. Jones's* is in the Genitive Case, so in Latin we often sandwich the Genitive between the Preposition and the Case which the Preposition governs.

EXERCISE 54.

THEMISTOCLES, A GREAT GREEK STATESMAN

Owing to the foresight of Themistocles, the Athenians built a large fleet. In a sea battle off the island of Salamis, opposite Athens, they won a victory, in 480 B.C., which saved Greece from the Persians. But for this victory the history of Europe would have been quite different.

Themistocles incolas Athenarum incitat et nautas ad pugnam parat; Xerxes enim cum copiis instat. Xerxes in Persis regnat; Persas ad Graeciam trans undas transportat. Persae praeter oram Thraciae et Thessaliae navigant. Procellae Persas vexant et ad oram iactant. Tandem incolae Graeciae Persas prope insulam exspectant pugnamque parant. Xerxes cum nautis non pugnat, sed ab ora spectat copiasque aut laudat aut incitat. Incolae tamen Graeciae Persas superant et victoriam pro patria reportant. Ita Themistocles per prudentiam Athenas conservat.

Words:

Athēnae, (pl.) *Athens.*
ad, here, *for the purpose of.*
in, here, *over.*
Persae, *the Persians.*
regnō, *I reign, am king.*
Graecia, *Greece.*
unda, *wave.*

Thrācia, *Thrace,* a country north of the Aegean Sea.
Thessalia, *Thessaly,* a country in the N.E. of Greece.
vexō, *I distress.*
prō (with Abl.), *on behalf of, for.*
prūdentia, *foresight.*

EXERCISE 55.

1. The Persians' forces are approaching the island.
2. After dinner we do not swim.

3. Why are you (s.) hurrying along the shore?
4. We are going into the house on account of the rain.
5. The troops are at length sailing to Gaul.
6. The cows are wandering through the wood.
7. Before the door of the cottage stands a cow.
8. Boadicea rouses the natives on behalf of their country.
9. The troops are fighting on the island against the Druids.
10. A little boat is approaching across the waves.

rain, **pluvia**.   *Gaul*, **Gallia**.

EXERCISE 56.

The forces of the Persians hurry towards Greece through Thrace and Thessaly. The inhabitants of Thessaly give to the Persians earth and water,[1] but Leonidas with his forces fights against the Persians in the pass of Thermopylae: he does not, however, drive back the Persians. Meanwhile Themistocles makes ready his sailors for battle near Athens. There they rout and defeat the Persians and so save their country.

Words:

Leonidas, **Leōnidās** (a king of Sparta).

pass, **angustiae** (pl.).

Thermopylae, **Thermopylae** (pl.).

meanwhile, **interim**.

[1] Earth and water were given as a sign of surrender.

Additional Exercises on the Accusative with Prepositions:

EXERCISE 57.

1. Copiae trans fossam properant.
2. Ante pugnam sagittas paramus.
3. Caesar copias ob procellam revocat.
4. Druidae feminas contra copias armant.
5. Vaccae aquam prope casam potant.
6. Cur Caesar copias ad Britanniam transportat?
7. Incolas per Britanniam superamus.
8. In fossam properamus, quod advenae appropinquant.
9. Vacca ad silvam appropinquat, nec tamen intrat.
10. Insidias post silvam paramus.

EXERCISE 58.

1. Hurry (pl.) to the shore.
2. We do not fight against our native land.
3. Do you (s.) fall asleep after dinner?
4. The troops are approaching through the gate.
5. We are sailing along the coast.
6. The farmer lives near Rome.
7. The women are hurrying to the wood because of the battle.
8. Druids live across the Severn.
9. Wild animals roam throughout the island.
10. After the battle the sailors announce the victory.

Place: *to, from, at,* with Proper Names

(1) **Cōpiae Rōmam festīnant.**
The troops hurry to Rome.

When a Proper Noun is used, giving the actual name of a town or small island, the Accusative without a Preposition is used to express *to* (of motion). The Roman standard of the size of islands was judged by Rhodes, which was taken as the largest small island and the smallest large island.

So: **Paulus Melitam nāvigat.**
Paul sails to Malta.
(But **ad Siciliam,** *to Sicily.*)

Similarly the Ablative is used without a Preposition to express *from*:

Persae Athēnīs festīnant.
The Persians hasten from Athens.

Cōpiās Monā revocat.
He recalls the troops from Anglesey.

(2) **Rōmae habitāmus.**
We live in Rome.

Rōmae is in a special Case, called the **Locative,** used with Proper Nouns, to express *at* or *in* towns and small islands.

The Locative Plur. of the 1st Declension ends in **-īs.**

So: **Puella Capreīs cēnat** (Nom. **Capreae**).
   The girl is dining in (the isle of) Capri.
   (But **in insulā cēnat,** *is dining in the island.*)

The Locative Sing. of the 1st Decl. ends in **-ae;**
the Locative Plur. of the 1st Decl. ends in **-īs.**

EXERCISE 59.

1. Persae Athenas navigant.
2. Romam appropinquamus.
3. Copiae Roma festinant.
4. Monam navigamus.
5. Nonne Devae habitas?
6. Nauta Dubris ad Galliam navigat.
7. Nautae vaccas Melitam transportant.
8. Athenas Roma migrat.
9. Advenae ad Siciliam appropinquant.
10. Themistocles Athenis habitat.

Dēva, *Chester.*   **migrō,** *I migrate, move.*
Dubrae (pl.), *Dover.*   **Sicilia,** *Sicily.*
Melita, *Malta.*

EXERCISE 60.

1. Recall (s.) the troops to Rome.
2. The girl is sailing to Capri.
3. Why are the troops hurrying from Chester?
4. We do not live in Rome.
5. The Persians are fighting at Thermopylae.
6. Where are they sailing to from Sicily?
7. Druids live in Anglesey.
8. The farmer carries hay into Silchester.
9. Why do you not live on the island?
10. I am moving to Chester from Anglesey.

   Capri, **Capreae** (pl.),   *Silchester,* **Callēva.**

Verbs with two Accusatives

A few Verbs of *hiding* and *asking* may take two Accusatives.

one of the *person*, and one of the *thing*, e.g. **cēlō**, *I hide*; **flāgitō**, *I demand*; **ōrō**, *I beg*; also **rogō**, *I ask*, when followed by **sententiam**, *opinion*:

Incolae pecūniam cōpiās cēlant.
The natives hide money from the troops.

Agricolam vaccās flāgitant.
They are demanding cows from the farmer.

Aquam incolās ōrāmus.
We are begging the natives for water.

Rēgīnamne sententiam rogās?
Are you asking the queen for her opinion?

EXERCISE 61.

(*a*) 1. Cacus vaccas advenam celat.
2. Nautae incolas insulae aquam flagitant.
3. Boudicca incolas sententiam rogat.
4. Nonne agricola praedam copias celat?
5. Reginam veniam orate.

sententia, *opinion.*

(*b*) 1. Why do you (s.) not ask the farmer his opinion?
2. The deserter is begging the lady for money.
3. How many cows are you (pl.) hiding from the troops?
4. Boadicea demands justice from the troops.
5. The farmer's daughter hides the hens from the strangers.

lady, **mātrōna.** *justice,* **iustitia.**

Derivation Test

1. Emigrate. 2. Transport. 3. Sentence. 4. Contrary.

Chapter 10

Complete 1st Declension and Revision Exercises

Here is a complete plan of the 1st Declension, showing the use of the Cases:

Base   naut-

Singular			*Use*
Nom.	**nauta**	*a sailor*	as Subject.
Voc.	**nauta**	*o sailor*	for addressing a *sailor*.
Acc.	**nautam**	*a sailor*	(i) as Direct Object; (ii) after certain Prepositions, including those used for Motion *towards*.
Gen.	**nautae**	*of a sailor*	for expressing *of*.
Dat.	**nautae**	*to* or *for a sailor*	(i) as Indirect Object (but not for *to* of Motion); (ii) to express *for* someone's Advantage.
Abl.	**nautā**	(*with, by, from, in*) *a sailor*	(i) without a Preposition, to express *instrument with which* you do something; (ii) with Prepositions, to express *in company with*; *from, out of*; *in*; *on*.

Plural			
Nom.	**nautae**	*sailors*	
Voc.	**nautae**	*o sailors*	
Acc.	**nautās**	*sailors*	The use of the Plural is the same as that of the Singular.
Gen.	**nautārum**	*of sailors*	
Dat.	**nautīs**	*to* or *for sailors*	
Abl.	**nautīs**	(*with, by, from, in*) *sailors*	

Notes:

1. The Accusative is used without a Preposition with named towns and small islands to express Motion *to*, and the Ablative in the same way to express Motion *from*.

2. The Locative of the 1st Decl. ends in -ae in the Sing., e.g. **Rōmae**, *at Rome*, and in -īs in the Plur., e.g. **Athenīs**, *at Athens*.

3. **Fīlia**, *daughter*, **dea**, *goddess*, have Dat. and Abl. Plur. **fīliābus**, **deābus**, to distinguish them from **fīliīs**, **deīs**, which come from 2nd Decl., Nouns, meaning *sons*, *gods*.

4. Nouns, like Verbs, have Stems, and the Stem of **nauta** is **nautā-**, but in the 1st Declension it is sufficient to consider the Base of a Noun, e.g. **naut-**.

EXERCISE 62.

1. In villa prope Devam habitamus.
2. Copiae ad oram Britanniae appropinquant.
3. Cur vaccae speluncam retro intrant?
4. Propter copiam aquae coloniam hic collocamus.
5. Persae Thermopylis Athenas properant.
6. Terram et aquam ab incolis postulant.
7. Num hastis et sagittis amicitiam confirmamus?
8. Vaccas celate, quod copiae appropinquant.
9. Druidae aram in silva aedificant.
10. Nautae gloriam reciperant, quod victoriam reportant.

    hĭc, *here*.   **glōria**, *renown*.

EXERCISE 63.

BRITAIN UNDER AGRICOLA

Agricola was governor of Britain for seven years from A.D. *77 or 78. He did much to Romanise the province and enlarged it by his victories in the north. Central and southern Scotland were occupied by the Romans till well into the reign of Trajan, whose successor Hadrian in about* A.D. *122 built a great wall from the Tyne to the Solway as the northern boundary.*

Agricola incolas Britanniae propter iustitiam conciliat et

provinciam bene administrat. Villis et balneis et luxuria epu-
iarum neque hastis incolas superat. Incolae etiam pro Agricolae copiis pugnant.

Agricola copias Clanoventae, ubi ora Britanniae ad Hiberniam spectat, collocat nec tamen ad Hiberniam transportat.
Usque ad Clotam et Bodotriam terram penetrat. Nautae
praeter oram Caledoniae navigant praedamque una cum copiis
saepe comparant. Procul a provincia Agricola copias ante
pugnam incitat. Primum copiae essedas fugant; deinde incolae
copiarum turbam paene circumdant. Tum quattuor alae a
dextra et a sinistra incolas oppugnant. Inde copiae incolas
ubique trucidant.

Words:

prōvincia, *province.*
bene, *well.*
administrō, *I govern.*
luxuria, *luxury.*
epulae (pl.), *feast, feasts.*
Clānoventa, *Ravenglass* (in
  Cumberland).
ubi, *where.*
Hibernia, *Ireland.*
spectō ad, *I look towards,
  face.*
usque ad, *as far as.*
Clōta, *Clyde.*

Bodotria, *Firth of Forth.*
penetrō, *I penetrate.*
ūnā, *together.*
procul, *far.*
quattuor, *four.*
āla, *wing of cavalry.*
ā dextrā, *on* (literally *from*) *the
  right.*
ā sinistrā, *on the left.*
inde, *then, from that time.*
ubīque, *everywhere.*
trucīdō, *I butcher.*

EXERCISE 64.

1. Agricola's troops are penetrating the country as far as
   the Clyde.
2. Sometimes the inhabitants of Britain fight for Agricola.
3. Where are you (pl.) sailing to from Ireland?
4. The forces are spending the winter far from Italy.
5. Agricola wins renown in Britain because of his kindness.
6. They are building a country-house at Ravenglass near
   the shore.
7. Banquets and baths please the inhabitants of the settlement.

8. Attack (pl.) on the right as far as the wood.
9. Dover faces France.
10. Agricola stations troops along the coast of Scotland.

EXERCISE 65.

By means of justice and kindness Agricola wins over the natives of Britain. He then hastens beyond Chester towards Scotland. He rouses his troops to battle and to victory. At first Agricola lays waste the land, then he displays to the natives his moderation. The troops penetrate Scotland, not only by land but also along the coast, as far as the Forth and the Clyde. Agricola overcomes the natives of Scotland; soon, however, Domitian[1] recalls Agricola to Rome.

Words:

beyond, **ultrā** (with Acc.).	*. . .* **sed etiam.**
moderation, **modestia.**	*Domitian,* **Domitiānus.**
not only . . . but also, **nōn modo**	

[1] Domitian was Emperor A.D. 81-96. Troops were now needed on the Danube frontier. The historian, Tacitus, who married Agricola's daughter, wrote a biography of his father-in-law and states that his recall was due to Domitian's jealousy.

Derivation Test

1. **Prōvincia.**   2. **Administrō.**   3. **Modestia.**   4. **Luxuria.**

Chapter 11

1st Conjugation: Future and Imperfect Indicative Active

	Future Tense			*Imperfect Tense*	
Sing.	amā-bō,	I shall love.		amā-bam,	I was loving,
	amā-bis,	you will love.		amā-bās	used to love,
	amā-bit,	he will love.		amā-bat	continued to
Plur.	amā-bimus,	we shall love.		amā-bāmus	love, began
	amā-bitis,	you will love.		amā-bātis	to love, etc.
	amā-bunt,	they will love.		amā-bant	

The various ways of translating an Imperfect Tense (see above) should be carefully noticed. The Imperfect is used for **continuous** action as contrasted with action that is **completed** at a particular point in time. **Nāvigābam** shows that *I went on sailing*; for *I sailed*, i.e. *I completed a voyage*, Latin uses the Perfect Tense, which will be met later.

Latin is far more exact than English in the use of Tenses. In *When I was a child, I spake as a child* Latin would express *I spake* by an Imperfect, because *I spake* really means *I used to speak, I went on speaking*. Care must be taken in translating Tenses from Latin into English, but even more care in choosing the right Latin Tense, when we translate English into Latin.

EXERCISE 66.

(*a*)
1. Aedifica-bit.
2. Ambula-bimus.
3. Erra-bunt.
4. Oppugna-bo.
5. Naviga-bitis.
6. Propera-bitis.

(*b*)
1. He will blame.
2. I will ask.
3. You (pl.) will announce.
4. They will carry.
5. We will stand.
6. You (s.) will prepare.

(*c*) 1. Porta-bant.   (*d*) 1. We were spending the winter.
    2. Clama-bam.   2. You (pl.) were hoping.
    3. Roga-bat.   3. I was approaching.
    4. Pugna-batis.   4. He continued to reign.
    5. Naviga-bamus.   5. You (s.) used to work.
    6. Despera-bas.   6. They began to build.

EXERCISE 67.

Translate Exercises 45 and 41 substituting the Future for the Present Tense (omitting any sentences with Verbs in the Imperative).

EXERCISE 68.

Translate Exercises 49 and 55 substituting the Imperfect for the Present Tense.

2nd Conjugation: Present, Future, and Imperfect Indicative Active

Present Tense	*Future Tense*	*Imperfect Tense*
S. **mone-ō,** *I advise* or	**monē-bō,** *I shall*	**monē-bam,** *I was ad-*
monē-s *warn,* etc.	**monē-bis** *advise,*	**monē-bās** *vising,*
mone-t	**monē-bit** etc.	**monē-bat** etc.
Pl. **monē-mus**	**monē-bimus**	**monē-bāmus**
monē-tis	**monē-bitis**	**monē-bātis**
mone-nt	**monē-bunt**	**monē-bant**

The 2nd Conjugation has an E- Stem. The endings are the same as those of the 1st Conjugation, but the 1st person sing. of the Present Tense of the 2nd Conjugation retains the Stem vowel.

Here are some Verbs of the 2nd Conjugation:

habeō, *I have.*   **timeō,** *I fear.*   **respondeō,** *I reply.*
teneō, *I hold.*   **rīdeō,** *I laugh, smile.*   **dēleō,** *I destroy.*
maneō, *I remain.*   **videō,** *I see.*   **exerceō,** *I train*
                                                           (trans.).

EXERCISE 69.

(a)
1. Tenemus.
2. Habet.
3. Monebant.
4. Videbimus.
5. Exercebam.
6. Respondes.
7. Timetis.
8. Manebis.
9. Delent.
10. Ridesne?

(b)
1. You (pl.) see.
2. We are training.
3. We will not fear.
4. He used to stay.
5. You (s.) have.
6. They began to laugh.
7. He was destroying.
8. I will advise.
9. You (pl.) were holding.
10. We do not reply.

(c)
1. Ridebamus.
2. Num times?
3. Delebis.
4. Monebas.
5. Respondebo.
6. Manebunt.
7. Non habetis.
8. Exercent.
9. Nonne vides?
10. Non tenebis.

(d)
1. He is smiling.
2. You (s.) will warn.
3. You (pl.) began to fear.
4. They have not.
5. We will remain.
6. He continued to train.
7. I was laughing.
8. They see.
9. They began to destroy.
10. Surely he is not laughing?

EXERCISE 70.

1. Copiae neque Druidas neque feminas timebant.
2. Agricola copias in Britannia exercebat.
3. Aras Druidarum delebimus.
4. Copiae Boudiccae villas delebant, coloniam vastabant.
5. Provinciam per victorias augemus.
6. Quod reginam timebat, Suetonius in insula non diu manebat.
7. Incolae hastas dextris tenebant.
8. Quod linguam ignoramus, non respondemus.
9. Da pecuniam filiae, quod non habet.
10. Propter iniurias incolae non ridebant, sed tacebant.

augeō, *I increase* (trans.).   **ignōrō,** *I do not know.*
lingua, *language.*   **taceō,** *I am silent.*

Exercise 71.

CHARIOT-FIGHTING IN BRITAIN

Incolae Britanniae ex essedis pugnabant. Primo passim perequitabant; non modo hastis sed etiam rotis essedarum copias terrebant; ita turmas penetrabant et perturbabant. Deinde subito de essedis evolabant et comminus pugnabant. Interim aurigae e pugna essedas paulatim removebant nec procul collocabant; ita fugam semper parabant.

Words:

passim, *in all directions.*
perequitō, *I drive about.*
rota, *wheel.*
terreō, *I frighten.*
turma, *squadron* (of cavalry).
subitō, *suddenly.*
dē (with Abl.), *down from.*

ēvolō, *I spring forth.*
comminus, *hand to hand.*
aurīga, *charioteer.*
paulātim, *gradually.*
removeō, *withdraw* (trans.).
fuga, *flight, escape.*

Exercise 72.

1. The inhabitants of Britain used to build their country-houses near water.
2. After the victory Agricola's troops were smiling.
3. Agricola remained in Britain for a long time.
4. Soon you (pl.) will again see Italy and Rome.
5. Because they are demanding money, the farmer does not reply to the troops.
6. The natives were destroying the colony with flames.
7. We will warn the troops about the ambush.
8. The women were removing the cows into the woods.
9. Because he works, the farmer increases his wealth.
10. Suetonius prepares his forces, because the Druids are holding Anglesey.

   about, dē (with Abl.).   *wealth,* dīvitiae (pl.).

Exercise 73.

The natives were hiding their chariots in a wood and preparing an ambush. Soon the troops were approaching. Suddenly the natives began to hurry out of the wood and drive about in all directions. The cavalry squadrons did not endure the fight for long, because they feared both the spears of the natives and the wheels of the chariots. Soon, therefore, Caesar began to call back his troops from the fight.

Words:

I endure, **sustineō**.

therefore, **igitur** (always 2nd word in clause).

2nd Conjugation: Imperative Active

The 2nd pers. sing. of the Imperative Active of **moneō** is **monē**, and the 2nd pers. plur. is **monēte**.

EXERCISE 74.

(a) 1. Ridete, puellae.
2. Mane in fossa.
3. Tace, o filia.
4. Sustinete pugnam.
5. Reginae respondete.

(b) 1. Remove (s.) the booty.
2. Hold (pl.) the island.
3. Train the troops, Agricola.
4. Fear (pl.) the queen's anger.
5. Destroy (pl.) the little boats.

Derivation Test

(a) 1. **Timeō.** 3. **Lingua.** 5. **Fuga.** 7. **Dēleō.**
2. **Rota.** 4. **Ignōrō.** 6. **Moneō.** 8. **Teneō.**

(b) 1. Response. 3. Permanent. 5. Terrible. 7. Sustain.
2. Exercise. 4. Removal. 6. Insidious. 8. Deride.

Chapter 12

2nd Declension: Nouns in **-us** and **-er**

The Stem of the 2nd Declension ends in **o-**, but it is sufficient to consider the Base and the endings.

Base	domin- *master (of* *household).*	magistr- *master* *(of school).*	puer- *boy.*
Sing.			
Nom.	**dominus**	**magister**	**puer**
Voc.	**domine**	**magister**	**puer**
Acc.	**dominum**	**magistrum**	**puerum**
Gen.	**dominī**	**magistrī**	**puerī**
Dat.	**dominō**	**magistrō**	**puerō**
Abl.	**dominō**	**magistrō**	**puerō**
Plur.			
Nom.	**dominī**	**magistrī**	**puerī**
Voc.	**dominī**	**magistrī**	**puerī**
Acc.	**dominōs**	**magistrōs**	**puerōs**
Gen.	**dominōrum**	**magistrōrum**	**puerōrum**
Dat.	**dominīs**	**magistrīs**	**puerīs**
Abl.	**dominīs**	**magistrīs**	**puerīs**

Like **dominus** are declined: **servus**, *slave*; **captīvus**, *prisoner*; **amīcus**, *friend*; **socius**, *ally*; **fīlius**, *son* (Voc. s. **fīlī** and Gen. s. **fīlī** or **fīliī**); **deus**, *god* (Voc. s. **deus**).

Like **magister** are declined: **ager**, *field*; **liber**, *book*; **faber**, *smith, workman*.

Like **puer** are declined: **socer**, *father-in-law*; **gener**, *son-in-law*; **līberī** (pl. only) *children.* **Vesper**, *evening* is found in the Acc. and Gen. sing. **Vir**, *man*, keeps **vir-** throughout.

75

Vocabularies

From this point onwards the Latin-English Vocabulary at the end of the book may be used for finding out the meaning of new Latin words, but before the Vocabulary is consulted, an intelligent guess should be made, founded on (a) knowledge of grammar, and (b) the sense of the rest of the sentence.

There is also an English-Latin Vocabulary.

EXERCISE 75.

1. Servi in agris pro domino laborant.
2. Puer magistro respondebat.
3. Agricola et servi murum aedificabant.
4. Incolae aras deis consecrabant.
5. Tacitus[1] victorias soceri narrabat.
6. Captivos a catenis liberabamus.
7. Regina cum sociis ad coloniam properat.
8. Captivi in silva manent ; vesperum exspectant.
9. Magister libros amicis saepe dabat.
10. Fabri hastas copiis Agricolae parant.

[1] See historical note on Exercise 65.

EXERCISE 76.

CARACTACUS CHALLENGES THE ROMANS

Caratacus (generally, though wrongly, called Caractacus) was a son of Cunobelinus who had reigned at Camulodūnum (Colchester) over the Trinobantes and most of south-east Britain. When the Romans captured Camulodunum, he organised resistance among the Ordovices in north and central Wales. It was probably in A.D. 51 *that Caratacus staked everything on a single battle in south Shropshire against Ostōrius Scapula, governor of Britain* A.D. 47-52.

Caratacus muros in clivo aedificat et copias praeter muros collocat. Inter Romanos et barbaros fluvius iacet. Barbari ante pugnam per deos iurant et victoriam orant. Ostorius locum explorabat; et clivos et barbarorum turbam timebat, copiae tamen pugnam postulabant. Subito trans fluvium cum

copiis properat. Primo barbari Romanos sagittis propulsant;
deinde Romani muros deturbant et barbaros adversus clivum
fugant; barbari enim neque loricas neque galeas habent.

Romani Caratacum Romam transportant. Hic inter captivos Caratacus ante oculos populi ambulat. Claudius Cara-
taco et propinquis veniam dat, in custodia tamen retinet.

Historic Present

Exercise 76 is the first piece of continuous Latin in which
both the Present and the Imperfect Tenses are used. Later on,
use will be made of the Perfect Tense, corresponding to the
English *he built*, *he stationed*, etc. The Perfect Tense could be
substituted for most of the Present Tenses in this exercise, but
the best Latin writers often use the Present Tense when
describing completed actions in the past, for the sake of vivid-
ness or variety. The Imperfect Tense, however, always refers
to continuous action.

EXERCISE 77.

1. The gods of the Britons do not frighten the Romans.
2. The messenger began to announce the victory to the
   prisoners.
3. The masters will train the boys on the playing-field.
4. How many workmen is Agricola transporting to Britain?
5. Look after the children, my son.
6. Agricola began to win over allies through his moderation.
7. The boys are carrying books for the master.
8. The schoolmaster was sailing to France with four friends.
9. The slaves will remove the cows from the fields.
10. The women call the men to dinner.

EXERCISE 78.

Caractacus seizes a hill and strengthens his position for
battle with walls. Between the hill and the Romans lies a river.
The river does not for long delay the Romans. Soon they were
climbing the hill, but the Britons began to drive back the
Romans towards the river. Then the Romans again climb the

slope; they now attack the Britons with swords and soon
overthrow the walls. They butcher the troops of Caractacus on
all sides, because they have neither helmets nor breastplates.

Derivation Test

(*a*) 1. Mūrus.   3. Gladius.   5. Oculus.   7. Populus.
     2. Liber.   4. Custōdia.   6. Barbarī.   8. Dominus.

(*b*) 1. Social.   3. Amicable.   5. Declivity.   7. Filial.
     2. Servile.   4. Tardy.   6. Fabricate.   8. Puerile.

Chapter 13
2nd Declension: Neuter Nouns

Gender

In English we naturally distinguish three **Genders**, e.g. in *he, she, it.* In Latin every Noun has a Grammatical Gender, and is either (1) **masculine** or (2) **feminine** or (3) **neuter**, (i.e. neither masculine nor feminine) or (4) **common** (i.e. either masculine or feminine, such as **incola,** *inhabitant*).

Latin Nouns denoting a male are masculine, e.g. **nauta,** *sailor.*

Latin Nouns denoting a female are feminine, e.g. **fēmina,** *woman.*

Latin Nouns denoting things not living are either masculine or feminine or neuter.

Nearly all Nouns of the 1st Declension are feminine.
Nearly all Nouns of the 2nd Declension in **-us** and **-er** are masculine.

There are no neuter Nouns in the 1st Declension, but there are many in the 2nd Declension, which has a special form for them in the Nom., Voc., and Acc., both in the singular and in the plural.

Here is the Declension of such a neuter Noun:

Base   **bell-,** *war.*

	Sing.	*Plur.*
Nom.	bellum	bella
Voc.	bellum	bella
Acc.	bellum	bella
Gen.	bellī	bellōrum
Dat.	bellō	bellīs
Abl.	bellō	bellīs

Like **bellum** are declined: **oppidum,** *town*; **templum,** *temple*;

proelium, *battle*; **vallum**, *rampart*; **signum**, *signal*; and in the plural **castra**, *camp*; **arma**, *arms, weapons*.

Castrum (sing.) means *fort*, but is not so common as **castellum**, which is often used.

Neuter Nouns in **-ium**, e.g. **auxilium**, *help*, form Gen. s. in **-ī** or **-iī**, i.e. **auxilī** or **auxiliī**.

2nd Declension: Locative Case

The Locative Case of the 2nd Declension ends in **-ī** in the sing. and in **-īs** in the plur., e.g. **Corinthī**, *at Corinth* (**Corinthus**); **Londīniī**, *at London* (**Londīnium**); **Philippīs**, *at Philippi* (**Philippī**, pl.); **humī**, *on the ground* (**humus**, f.).

Intransitive Verbs used with a Dative

There are some Verbs in Latin which are Intransitive, i.e. do not have a Direct Object in the Accusative, but which do not give complete sense by themselves. Among such Verbs are: **noceō**, *I am harmful*; **pāreō**, *I am obedient*; **placeō**, *I am pleasing*. In Latin, a Dative is used to complete their sense; in English we often represent these Verbs by Transitive Verbs, *I hurt, I obey, I please*:

Britannī Agricolae pārēbant.
The Britons used to obey Agricola.

Verb with two Accusatives

Like certain Verbs of *hiding* and *asking*, **doceō**, *I teach*, may be used with two Accusatives:

Magister puerōs litterās docet.
The master is teaching the boys their letters.

Exercise 79.
1. Romani templum Claudio Camuloduni consecrant.
2. Iceni bellum contra Romanos movebant.
3. Fabri theatrum Verulami aedificant.
4. Musicamne filiam doces?
5. Britanni vinum et oleum a Gallia importabant.
6. Imperium Romanorum Britannis non semper placebat.

7. Britanni praefectis parent, si oppida bene administrant.
8. Castra vallo et fossa circumdate.
9. Romani socios ad arma vocabant.
10. Caratacus copias ad proelium parat.

EXERCISE 80.

HONOUR BEFORE ADVANTAGE

From 280 to 275 B.C. the Romans were at war with Pyrrhus, King of Ēpīrus (a country south of Macedonia on the east coast of the Adriatic). He invaded Italy from the south and advanced as far as Latium. Fābricius, who took an important part in driving Pyrrhus out of Italy, became known as the type of Roman who held that nothing can be advantageous that is not honourable.

Pyrrhus bellum contra Romanos movet. Populus Fabricio imperium copiarum mandat. Perfuga castra Fabricii clam intrat. 'Si, Fabrici',[1] inquit[2] 'praemium dabis, Pyrrhi castra clam intrabo et Pyrrhum veneno necabo.' Filius enim perfugae vinum Pyrrho semper ministrabat. Fabricius consilium repudiat; armis enim, non veneno Romani certant. Populus Fabricium laudat, quod flagitium vitat.

[1] **Fābricius** and many proper names in **-ius** have Voc. in **-ī**, like **filius**.
[2] **inquit**, *says he*, always placed after one or two words of the speaker.

EXERCISE 81.
1. How many languages do the masters teach the boys?
2. Suetonius hurries to London from Anglesey.
3. The Romans attack the Druids, when the commander gives the signal.
4. Caractacus began to strengthen the position with stones.
5. The Romans continued to build forts throughout Britain.
6. The Romans do not harm the Britons, if they are obedient.
7. The smiths were getting ready the arms for war.
8. The commander rouses the troops before the battle.

F

9. The Britons built towns on hills, the Romans near rivers.
10. Agricola did not stay long in the camp.

EXERCISE 82.

Pyrrhus brings his troops across the Adriatic to Italy and gains victories[1] near Heraclea and at Ausculum. He fights for a long time both in Italy and in Sicily. But he did not guard[2] against dangers. Pyrrhus's doctor prepares a plan and secretly hurries to Fabricius. 'I will give Pyrrhus poison', says he, 'in return for a reward.' But the plan does not please Fabricius, because Romans do not gain power by poison.

[1] He lost so many men that a *Pyrrhic* victory has become proverbial.
[2] Use **caveō** (with Acc.)

Derivation Test

(a) 1. **Castellum.**   3. **Littera.**   5. **Arma.**
      2. **Imperium.**   4. **Medicus.**   6. **Theātrum.**

(b) 1. Musician.   3. Counsel.   5. Doctrine.
      2. Prefect.   4. Bellicose.   6. Sign.

Chapter 14

Adjectives of 1st and 2nd Declensions in -us, -a, -um

Agreement of Adjectives

An **Adjective** means a word that is *fit for adding* to a Noun. When it is added to a Noun, it defines the Noun more clearly, e.g. *small island*, *Roman power*.

English Adjectives do not change their endings when they are added to Nouns: in *old man*, *old ladies*, *of old trees*, the Adjective *old* remains unchanged.

In Latin the Adjective has to be made fit to be added to the Noun in three ways: it must agree with its Noun in **Gender, Number,** and **Case.**

Adjectives in Latin, then, are declined.

Here is the plan of an Adjective of which the masculine is declined like **dominus,** the feminine like **mensa,** and the neuter like **bellum:**

Base   **bon-,** *good.*

Sing.	Masc.	Fem.	Neut.
Nom.	bonus	bona	bonum
Voc.	bone	bona	bonum
Acc.	bonum	bonam	bonum
Gen.	bonī	bonae	bonī
Dat.	bonō	bonae	bonō
Abl.	bonō	bonā	bonō
Plur.			
Nom.	bonī	bonae	bona
Voc.	bonī	bonae	bona
Acc.	bonōs	bonās	bona
Gen.	bonōrum	bonārum	bonōrum
Dat.	bonīs	bonīs	bonīs
Abl.	bonīs	bonīs	bonīs

Like **bonus** are declined: **magnus**, *great*, *large*; **parvus**
small; **altus**, *high*, *deep*; **densus**, *thick;* **antīquus**, *ancient*;
multus, *much* (mostly found in pl. for *many*); **meus**, *my* (Voc.
sing. masc. **mī**); **tuus**, *your* (adjective of 2nd pers. sing.).

Order of Adjectives

Adjectives are more often placed *after* their Nouns than
before, but Adjectives expressing quantity such as **multus,**
much, are placed *before*, as in English.

> **Vir bonus multōs amīcōs habet.**
> *A good man has many friends.*

The rule that an Adjective must agree with its Noun in
Gender, Number, and Case is clearly shown in the above
example, and the Adjectives are placed in their normal position: **bonus** is Nom. masc. sing. to agree with **vir**, and is placed
after it; **multōs** is Acc. masc. plur. to agree with **amīcōs**, and is
placed before it, because it expresses quantity.

The Genders of Nouns are given in the Vocabularies at the
end of the book. Care should be taken with those Nouns of the
1st Decl. which are masc., e.g. **agricola** and **nauta**.

> **Agricola bonus equōs cūrat.**
> *A good farmer looks after his horses.*

EXERCISE 83.
1. Britanni essedas in silvis densis celabant.
2. Romani balneas magnas Viroconii aedificant.
3. Multi Britanni pro Agricola pugnabant.
4. Amicos meos ad cenam invitabo.
5. Fluvius altus copias tardabat.
6. Magna feminarum turba[1] tabernam parvam intrabat.
7. Romani oppida muris altis circumdabant.
8. Populus Romanus multa bella movebat.
9. Pyrrhus cum magnis copiis ad Italiam appropinquat.
10. Murumne oppidi antiqui spectatis?

[1] This is the usual order when a Noun is joined with both an
Adjective and a Genitive.

EXERCISE 84.

ROMULUS TAKEN UP TO HEAVEN

Livy, the Roman historian (59 B.C. to A.D. 17) records the story that Rōmulus, the traditional founder of Rome in 753 B.C., did not die a natural death, but was taken up into heaven.

Titus Livius fabulam miram de Romulo narrat. Romulus in Campo Martio copias magnas recensebat et in solio regio sedebat. Subito caelum resonat; procella magna Romulum nimbo denso celat. Ubi iterum lucet,[1] Romani ad Romulum spectant, sed solium vacuum vident. Miraculum dirum Romanos diu terrebat; inde Romani Romulum in numero deorum habebant Romulumque auxilium pro populo Romano orabant.

[1] **lūcet,** from **lūceō,** *I shine.* Here the 3rd pers. sing. is used Impersonally, i.e. without a Personal Subject, and means *it is light.* Compare in English, *it is raining.*

EXERCISE 85.

1. Where will you (s.) have dinner with your friends?
2. Many arms were lying in the ditch.
3. The thick wood will conceal large forces.
4. A big crowd of boys is waiting for the masters.
5. Teach (s.) the boys ancient languages.
6. Why does the boy not obey my advice?
7. Many Britons used to live in little huts.
8. Large forces began to hurry to London.
9. My friends live in a little country-house.
10. Why do you (s.) surround your garden with a high wall?

EXERCISE 86.

Large forces enter the field of Mars. Here Romulus sits on the royal throne and reviews the troops. Suddenly a thick mist darkens the plain; when the Romans again look towards the throne, Romulus no longer appears before their eyes. The Romans began to be afraid on account of the terrible wonder and were silent for a long time; then, as Livy relates, they began to worship Romulus.

Derivation Test

(*a*) 1. Antiquus.   3. Numerus.   5. Magnus.
    2. Altus.   4. Mīrāculum   6. Multus.

(*b*) 1. Invitation.   3. Evacuate.   5. Equine.
    2. Density.   4. Auxiliary.   6. Martian.

Chapter 15

Adjectives of 1st and 2nd Declension in -er, -a, -um

In the following type of Adjective the Declension of the masculine follows that of **magister** and the Base is formed in the same way:

Base   **nigr-,** *black.*

Sing.	M.	F.	N.
Nom.	niger	nigra	nigrum
Voc.	niger	nigra	nigrum
Acc.	nigrum	nigram	nigrum
Gen.	nigrī	nigrae	nigrī
Dat.	nigrō	nigrae	nigrō
Abl.	nigrō	nigrā	nigrō
Plur.			
Nom.	nigrī	nigrae	nigra
Voc.	nigrī	nigrae	nigra
Acc.	nigrōs	nigrās	nigra
Gen.	nigrōrum	nigrārum	nigrōrum
Dat.	nigrīs	nigrīs	nigrīs
Abl.	nigrīs	nigrīs	nigrīs

Like **niger** are declined: **noster,** *our*; **vester,** *your* (adjective of 2nd pers. plur.); **pulcher,** *beautiful*; **sacer,** *sacred*; **aeger,** *sick*; **sinister,** *left*.

A few Adjectives keep -er throughout, like **puer:**

Base   **tener-,** *tender.*

Sing.	M.	F.	N.
Nom.	tener	tenera	tenerum
Voc.	tener	tenera	tenerum
Acc.	tenerum	teneram	tenerum
Gen.	tenerī	tenerae	tenerī

| Dat. | tenerō | tenerae | tenerō |
| Abl. | tenerō | tenerā | tenerō |

Plur.

Nom.	tenerī	tenerae	tenera
Voc.	tenerī	tenerae	tenera
Acc.	tenerōs	tenerās	tenera
Gen.	tenerōrum	tenerārum	tenerōrum
Dat.	tenerīs	tenerīs	tenerīs
Abl.	tenerīs	tenerīs	tenerīs

Like **tener** are declined: **asper**, *rough*; **līber**, *free*; **miser**, *wretched*; **lacer**, *torn*; **prosper**, *prosperous*.

Dexter, *right*, is generally declined like **niger**, but sometimes declined like **tener**.

The feminines of **dexter** and **sinister**, **dextra** and **sinistra**, are often used for *right hand, left hand*, a feminine Noun for *hand* (which will be met later) being understood. In English compare the expression in boxing, *he led with his right*. See Exercise 63 for the phrases **ā dextrā, ā sinistrā**, *on the right, on the left*.

Adjectives used as Nouns

The endings of the Latin Adjectives, -us or -er, -a, -um; -ī, -ae, -a, etc., express *man, woman, thing*, in the singular and the plural, and therefore some Adjectives are often used without Nouns:

bonī, *good men* or *the good.*
bona (neut. pl.), *goods.*
multī, *many men.*
multa, *many things.*
nostrī, *our men*, as opposed to *the enemy.*
paucī, *few men* (**paucus** in sing. very rare).
pauca, *few things.*

Two Adjectives with one Noun

When two Adjectives are used with one Noun, they follow the Noun and are joined by *et*[1]:

[1] Unless one of the Adjectives is a Possessive or Demonstrative, an Adjective of quantity, or a Numeral.

Templum pulchrum et antiquum intrāmus.
We are entering a beautiful old temple.

EXERCISE 87.
1. Copiae nostrae pericula non timebant.
2. Medicus bonus pueros aegros sanabit.
3. Via aspera et longa nostros tardat.
4. Agricola vaccas et albas et nigras habet.
5. Multi bona ex oppido in agros removebant.
6. Multi certant, pauci praemia comparant.
7. Hic Sacram Viam vides.
8. A dextra stat templum magnum et pulchrum.
9. Viri liberi patriam amant.
10. Fortuna prospera Romanos saepe iuvabat.

EXERCISE 88.

A SCOTTISH GENERAL DEFIES
THE ROMANS

Calgacus, a Caledonian chieftain, addresses his troops before battle. He was heavily defeated by Agricola at an unknown place called the Graupian Hill in A.D. 84. *According to Tacitus, 10,000 Caledonians fell in this battle, and only 360 Romans.*

'Hodie pro patria adhuc libera contra Romanos pugnabitis Patriam vestram in dextris vestris portatis. Num Romani agros nostros et bona vastabunt? Num liberos nostros in provincias longinquas transportabunt? Num servos dominis Romanis praebebimus? Multi Britanni pro Romanis pugnant, quod Agricola ita imperat; non modo igitur patriam, sed etiam socios per victoriam vestram liberabitis. Romani et vias et silvas ignorant; pauci contra multos certant. Properate in proelium et posteros vestros cogitate.'

EXERCISE 89.
1. The maid is preparing a small tender chicken for dinner.
2. The wretched prisoners were walking through the streets.
3. The natives began to attack our men on the left.
4. The commander was having dinner with a few friends.

5. The Greeks taught the Romans many things.
6. The doctor will look after the sick boys.
7. Obey (pl.) your commander.
8. Our allies were preparing many arms.
9. Our men were fighting in distant lands.
10. The big rough stones did not hinder our troops for long.

EXERCISE 90.

'Today with your arms you (pl.) will free Caledonia, soon you will free Britain. Drive back the Romans for the sake of[1] your children; for the Romans, when they conquer a province, demand slaves. Our forces will fight in their native land; the Romans will fight far from their relations. Besides, the Romans do not know the rough woods and roads. Many things therefore rouse our forces to victory, few things help the Romans. Among the Romans you will see our own allies; for the Britons will at once fight for our country, not for the Romans.'

[1] *for the sake of,* **causā,** placed after a Genitive.

Derivation Test

(*a*) 1. **Asper.**   2. **Lacer.**   3. **Sānō.**   4. **Sinister.**

(*b*) 1. Sacred.   2. Prosperity.   3. Miserable.   4. Dexterous.

Chapter 16

The Verb **sum**: Present, Future, and Imperfect Indicative

Present Tense	*Future Tense*	*Imperfect Tense*
S. sum, *I am.*	erō, *I shall be.*	eram, *I was.*
es, *you are.*	eris, *you will be*, etc.	erās, *you were*, etc.
est, *he, she, it, is.*	erit	erat
Pl. sumus, *we are.*	erimus	erāmus
estis, *you are.*	eritis	erātis
sunt, *they are.*	erunt	erant

Uses of sum

(1) The Verb **sum** is most commonly used as a link Verb between the Subject and either a Noun or an Adjective (or both): in this way the Verb together with the Noun or Adjective (or both) makes a statement about the Subject:

(a) **Gallī sunt sociī.**
The Gauls are allies.

(b) **Puer est bonus.**
The boy is good.

(c) **Mona est insula parva.**
Anglesey is a small island.

The Noun or Adjective which completes the sense of any part of **sum** is called its **Complement** and must always be in the same Case as the Subject; if it is an Adjective, it must also agree with the Subject in Number and Gender.

In example (a) above, **sociī** is Nom. because **Gallī** is Nom.

In example (b) above, **bonus** is Nom. because **puer** is Nom. It is also sing. and masc. in Gender, because **puer** is sing. and masc.

Example (c) follows example (a), except that here there is an Adjective in agreement with the Noun which follows the link Verb.

When **sum** is used as a link Verb, it is not generally placed at the end of the sentence.

Sometimes the Subject is not separately expressed, but is expressed in the Verb:

> **Praeclārus est propter sapientiam.**
> *He is famous on account of his wisdom.*

(2) **Sum** is also used with the meaning *I exist* or *I am* at a place or in a certain situation:

> **Sunt oppida pulchra in Britanniā.**
> *There are beautiful towns in Britain.*

> **In magnō perīculō sumus.**
> *We are in great danger.*

EXERCISE 91.

(a) 1. Arma nostra sunt antiqua.
  2. Londinium est oppidum magnum.
  3. Multae provinciae sunt longinquae.
  4. Nonne fessi estis?
  5. Verba Calgaci erant grata multis.
  6. Caledonia adhuc erat libera.
  7. Quod Romani appropinquant, non iam laeti sumus.
  8. Est forum magnum Romae.
  9. Verba praefecti erant clara, sed aspera.
  10. Incolae Verulamii non erunt tuti.

(b) 1. Num matura sunt poma?
  2. Silva non erat densa.
  3. Propter viam longam fessi sumus.
  4. Casae Britannorum erant parvae.
  5. Pauci Romani erant nautae.
  6. Fluvius non erat altus.
  7. Liber tuus est multis notus.
  8. Gratumne puero est donum?
  9. Victoria Romanis erat grata.
  10. Amicus meus est magister.

EXERCISE 92.

A MAGIC RING

Misuse of a discovery gives the kingdom of Lydia to the shepherd, Gȳges. Lydia was a country in Asia Minor. A native Lydian, called Gyges, actually did seize the kingdom in about 700 B.C.

Gyges erat Lydus. Quondam in agris errabat. Subito, ubi terra propter pluviam magnam hiat, cavernam videt. In cavernam statim properat Gyges, et, ut fabula narrat, equum aeneum videt; deinde equum intrat (in equo enim erat ianua) et virum maximum videt mortuum anulumque aureum in digito. Anulum digito suo aptat et e caverna ad amicos festinat. Natura anuli est mira. Si enim palam anuli ad palmam movet, nemo virum videt; si palam in locum solitum movet, amici virum rursus vident. Itaque Gyges per anulum et dominum et inimicos clam necat. Sic repente anuli beneficio regnum Lydiae comparat. Cicero fabulam narrat, nec tamen virum laudat; non enim erat honestus.

EXERCISE 93.

(a) 1. The sailors were not tired.
     2. The Roman temple was beautiful.
     3. The gifts will be welcome to the troops.
     4. Britain was a distant province.
     5. The goods of the inhabitants are not safe.
     6. The roads were broad and long.
     7. Your (s.) country-house is well-known to many.
     8. Is the new book welcome to the boys?
     9. Our cottage is small.
   10. The big apples were not ripe.

(b) 1. The garrison was safe.
     2. The Roman camp is big.
     3. The walls of the town are high.
     4. There are many troops in the camp.
     5. Their native land was dear to the Romans.
     6. The river was long, but not broad.
     7. Are you a farmer?

8. We are your (pl.) allies.
9. The commander's signal was not clear.
10. Great will be the victory.

EXERCISE 94.

In the cave there is a bronze horse and in the horse lies a very big man. Because the man is dead, Gyges is not in danger. He removes a golden ring from the finger of the dead man. Because he is not honourable, he obtains many things by the wonderful service of the ring. He kills his enemies and even his royal master. In this way he obtains the kingdom of Lydia. So great is the power[1] of greed.

[1] potentia.

Derivation Test

(a) 1. **Verbum.**   3. **Lātus.**   5. **Maximus.**
    2. **Nōtus.**   4. **Mātūrus.**   6. **Beneficium.**

(b) 1. **Janitor.**   3. **Donor.**   5. **Potentate.**
    2. **Clarity.**   4. **Local.**   6. **Digit.**

Chapter 17

Apposition

When a Noun is followed by another Noun in such a way that the second explains or describes the first, the second Noun agrees in Case with the first, and is said to be in Apposition to it:

Agricola, vir bonus, prōvinciam administrat.
Agricola, a good man, is governing the province.
Populus Rōmānus Caratacum, Britannum praeclārum, spectat.
The Roman people are looking at Caractacus, a famous Briton.

Where in English we say *the town of London, the island of Anglesey*, the Romans would say **oppidum Londīnium, insula Mona**, the name of the town and island being put in Apposition.

The Verb sum: Imperative

The 2nd pers. sing. of the Imperative of **sum** is **es** (**estō** is always used instead of **es**, but the **-es** form is regularly used in compounds of **sum**), and the 2nd pers. plur. is **este**:

Ades
Be present.

Laetī este, ō Rōmānī.
Be joyful, Romans.

Compounds of sum

Like **sum** are conjugated several compounds, e.g. **adsum**, *I am present*, **absum**, *I am absent, am distant*; **supersum**, *I am left over, survive*:

Puerī adsunt.
The boys are here.

Nōn multum absumus ā villā.
We are not far away from the house.

Sum with Dative of Possessor

Possession of something is often expressed in Latin by the use of **sum** followed by a Dat. of the person who possesses; the thing possessed is then the Subject and in the Nom. Case:

Erat Alexandrō equus.
Alexander had a horse.

EXERCISE 95.

1. Boudicca, regina barbara, adest.
2. Est magistro liber novus.
3. Gallos, socios nostros, iuvabamus.
4. Cur tot pueri hodie absunt?
5. Ad oppidum Londinium properamus.
6. Britannia multum abest ab Italia.
7. Servi agricolam, dominum bonum, salutant.
8. Londinium, oppidum magnum, filiam meam delectat.
9. Erant Britannis neque galeae neque loricae.
10. Romani Caledoniam, terram longinquam, penetrabant.

EXERCISE 96.

AENEAS LANDS IN ITALY

One Roman legend attributed the foundation of Rome to Aeneas. He was said to have migrated to Italy after the capture of Troy by the Greeks in 1183 B.C. This is an earlier legend than the one which made Romulus the founder of Rome.

Graeci Troiam, oppidum antiquum, longum[1] post bellum cremant. Inde Aeneas, filius Anchisae, multis[1] cum sociis ad Italiam migrat. Forte Troiani in agrum[2] Laurentinum, ubi regnabat Latinus, errant. Quod iam nihil praeter arma supererat, praedam ex agris comportabant. Incolae Troianos vident et arma ad proelium parant, sed subito Latinus praefectum advenarum ad colloquium evocat et multa rogat. Mox Aeneas respondet: 'Troiani sumus; filius sum Anchisae; domici-

[1] The Adjective is frequently separated from its Noun by a Preposition.
[2] ager here, as often, means *territory*.

lium oramus.' Latinus dat dextram et Aeneam in hospitium invitat; mox filiam Laviniam Aeneae dat in matrimonium.

EXERCISE 97.

1. My son has many friends.
2. Chester, an ancient town, is not far away.
3. We are glad because our friend is here.
4. Domitian is recalling Agricola, a good governor, because of envy.
5. Our troops remained in the town of Chester.
6. The girl lived in the isle of Capri.
7. The town of London was once on fire.
8. We are waiting for help from the Gauls, our allies.
9. Our friends have neither oil nor wine.
10. We were sailing on the Rhine, a beautiful river.

EXERCISE 98.

Many Trojans hurry to the shore without delay, because the town of Troy is on fire. Aeneas, son of Anchises, sails from Troy and wanders with his friends both to Africa and to the island of Sicily. At last, they approach Italy, a distant country. The Trojans have neither food nor a home. Latinus, the prince of the inhabitants, does not fight against the strangers. He gives territory to the Trojans, because they are wandering far from their native land; to Aeneas he gives in marriage his daughter, Lavinia.

Derivation Test

(*a*) 1. **Domicilium.** 2. **Regnō.** 3. **Novus.** 4. **Mātrimōnium.**

(*b*) 1. Colloquial. 2. Ardent. 3. Cremation. 4. Hospitable.

Chapter 18

Sentences for Revision

EXERCISE 99.

1. Magister pueros linguam Latinam docet.
2. Cur per agros nostros erratis?
3. Copiae Romanae castra Lindi locant.
4. Villa amici mei ad silvam pulchram spectat.
5. Britanni frumentum Romanos celabant.
6. Cavete, o pueri, pericula viarum latarum.
7. Servi boni bonis dominis parent.
8. Sunt amico tuo multae vaccae.
9. Claudius Caratacum, captivum praeclarum, Romae retinet.
10. Persae Athenas, oppidum antiquum, navigant.

EXERCISE 100.

1. The Britons had many chariots.
2. The Trojans began to beg Latinus for territory.
3. There were many temples, but few theatres in the island.
4. Caractacus, the commander of the Britons, strengthens his position with stones.
5. Dangers of war frighten even good commanders.
6. Aeneas was often in great danger.
7. Titus Livius tells many stories about the Romans.
8. There is a beautiful statue in the temple.
9. The Britons were preparing an ambush for our men in the wood.
10. Fabricius, an honourable man, rejects the wicked plan.

EXERCISE 101.

1. Et pueros et puellas linguam Graecam doceo.
2. Nostri Britannos a dextra oppugnabant.

3. Ubi villam filiae tuae aedificabis?
4. Iulia, ancilla bona, liberos meos curat.
5. Sunt magistro tuo multi libri.
6. Britanni Romanos iustitiam flagitant.
7. Gallia diu erat in magno periculo.
8. Cur praefectus noster signum non dat?
9. Propter nebulam densam non hodie navigabimus.
10. Bona vestra sub terra celate; Romani non multum absunt.

EXERCISE 102.
1. Agricola gives his daughter in marriage to Tacitus.
2. Gyges no longer appeared before the eyes of his friends.
3. Have you (s.) a ripe apple?
4. There is a large theatre at St. Albans.
5. Many deserters continued to approach our camp.
6. Few men were left to Pyrrhus after his victory.
7. The workmen will get the country-house ready for their master.
8. A large crowd of boys is hurrying to the playing-field.
9. My son, think of the words of good men.
10. There are good shops in Chester.

Chapter 19

1st and 2nd Conjugations: Perfect Indicative Active; Perfect Indicative of **sum**

All Perfect Tenses are formed by adding the endings **-ī, -istī, -it, -imus, -istis, -ērunt** to the Perfect Base of the Verb.

1st Conjugation	2nd Conjugation	**Sum**
Perfect Base		
amāv-	**monu-**	**fu-**
S. **amāv-ī,** *I loved*	**monu-ī,** *I advised*	**fu-ī,** *I was or have*
amāv-istī or *have*	**monu-istī** or *have*	**fu-istī** *been,* etc.
amāv-it *loved,*	**monu-it** *advised,*	**fu-it**
Pl. **amāv-imus** etc.	**monu-imus** etc.	**fu-imus**
amāv-istis	**monu-istis**	**fu-istis**
amāv-ērunt	**monu-ērunt**	**fu-ērunt**

The Latin Perfect Tense does the work of two English Tenses, (1) the ordinary Past Tense used in telling of past events and (2) the true Perfect Tense with *have*.

Librum cēlāvī, therefore, could mean either, (1) *I hid the book* (*at some time in the past*) or (2) *I have hidden the book* (*I have finished the act of hiding it and it is still hidden*).

The sense will generally make clear in which way a Latin Perfect Tense is used. An English Past Tense, however, if it refers to continuous or incomplete action, must be translated by an Imperfect Tense in Latin, e.g. **Tum Londīniī habitābam,** *at that time I lived in London.*

Where the Perfect Tense of a 1st or 2nd Conjugation Verb is used in the next few exercises, the Perfect Base is formed like that of **amō (amāv-)** or of **moneō (monu-),** according to the Conjugation of the Verb.

EXERCISE 103. (Both ways of translating a Latin Perfect Tense should be practised.)

(a) 1. Praefectus appropinquavit.
2. Castra oppugnavimus.
3. Ancillamne vocavisti?
4. Hic fuit oppidum.
5. Villam intraverunt.
6. Praedam comparavi.
7. Quot pueros docuisti?
8. Insulam non tenuimus.
9. Nauta multa narravit.
10. Pueri magistro paruerunt.

(b) 1. We have fought.
2. He was a good man.
3. I warned the boy.
4. Agricola transported the troops.
5. Has she been ill?
6. You (s.) prepared dinner for many.
7. The cow did not please the farmer.
8. You (pl.) have held back the corn.
9. We have trained the horses.
10. Many obtained booty.

EXERCISE 104.

(a) 1. Pugnam non sustinuimus.
2. Captivus veniam oravit.
3. Flammae villam vastaverunt.
4. Filiamne tuam sententiam rogavisti?
5. Ad insulam navigavimus.
6. Num victoriam speravistis?
7. Praefectus locum exploravit.
8. Diu regnum tenuit.
9. Britannia fuit quondam provincia.
10. Periculum non timuerunt.

(b) 1. There was once a camp here.
2. They obeyed the queen's words.
3. You have been silent, my friend.

4. I have been waiting for a letter.
5. Where did the maid hurry to?
6. We have worked for a long time.
7. How many cottages have you (pl.) built?
8. Cacus hoped for a big dinner.
9. I often entered the temple.
10. Where have you hidden the arms?

3rd Declension: Nouns with Consonant Stems, masculine and feminine

Nouns of the 3rd Declension fall into two main types. Of the first type are Nouns whose Stems end in a Consonant and with one more syllable in the Gen. sing. than in the Nom. sing.

Stem	rēg- *king* (m.)	mīlit- *soldier* (c.)	consul- *consul*[1] (m.)	leōn- *lion* (m.)
Sing.				
Nom.	rex	mīles	consul	leō
Voc.	rex	mīles	consul	leō
Acc.	rēgem	mīlitem	consulem	leōnem
Gen.	rēgis	mīlitis	consulis	leōnis
Dat.	rēgī	mīlitī	consulī	leōnī
Abl.	rēge	mīlite	consule	leōne
Plur.				
Nom.	rēgēs	mīlitēs	consulēs	leōnēs
Voc.	rēgēs	mīlitēs	consulēs	leōnēs
Acc.	rēgēs	mīlitēs	consulēs	leōnēs
Gen.	rēgum	mīlitum	consulum	leōnum
Dat.	rēgibus	mīlitibus	consulibus	leōnibus
Abl.	rēgibus	mīlitibus	consulibus	leōnibus

[1] Consuls, two in number, were the supreme magistrates in Rome, first elected after the expulsion of Kings in 510 B.C.

The Nom. and Voc. of masc. and fem. Nouns of this type have the same form; the other Cases are formed by adding the Case-endings, as shown above, to the Stem. The Gen. sing. of Nouns is given in the vocabulary and the Stem of a 3rd Decl.

Consonant Noun is easily found by taking away the Case-ending, -is, of the Gen. sing.

Like the above are declined: **vox, vōcis** (f.), *voice*; **dux, ducis** (c.), *leader*; **pedes, peditis** (m.), *foot-soldier* (pl. *infantry*); **eques, equitis** (m.), *horseman* (pl. *cavalry*); **sōl, sōlis** (m.), *sun*; **latrō, latrōnis** (m.) *robber*.

As the Gen. sing. of **vox** is **vōc-is**, the Stem of **vox** is **vōc-**; similarly the Stem of **pedes** is **pedit-**, etc.

The following three Nouns are also declined like the above, though they have the same number of syllables in the Gen. sing. as in the Nom. sing: **pater, patris** (m.), *father*; **māter, mātris** (f.), *mother*; **frāter, frātris** (m.), *brother*.

EXERCISE 105.

1. Milites locum non tenuerunt.
2. Rex victoriam militum laudavit.
3. Dux latronum praedam in silva celavit.
4. Aeneas cum patre et filio migravit.
5. Consules multa Romae administrabant.
6. Mox pedites equitibus auxilium dabant.
7. Vox magna magistri pueros non terruit.
8. Propter nebulam solem non videmus.
9. Erat consulibus magnum imperium.
10. Romani regibus imperium quondam mandabant.

EXERCISE 106.

HERCULES AND THE NEMEAN LION

One of the labours of Hercules, was the killing of the lion of Nemea. Nemea was a city in Greece, a little to the south-west of Corinth.

Leo saevus agros prope Nemeam, oppidum Argivum, vastabat; greges devorabat etiamque homines[1]; propter leonem incolae desperabant, nemo tamen necavit. Erat apud Eurystheum, regem Argivorum, Hercules, heros praeclarus. Eurystheus tamen Herculis virtuti semper invidebat; exitium Herculis

---

[1] **homō,** is *man* as opposed to *animal*; **vir** is *man* as opposed to *woman.*

potius quam leonis in animo parabat. Herculem igitur vocavit.
'Neca leonem,' inquit; 'virtutem tuam demonstra.'

Hercules, quod Eurystheus ita imperavit, Nemeam festin-
avit; incolae vestigia leonis monstraverunt. Sine mora Hercules
silvam, ubi latebat leo, penetravit. Subito apparuit leo.
Sagittae tamen contra leonem non valebant; ne clava quidem[1]
valebat; diu Hercules in latebris cum leone frustra certabat.
Denique tamen leonem strangulavit, tum ad Eurystheum
mortuum reportavit.

[1] **nē . . . quidem,** *not even*, with the word that is emphasized between them.

EXERCISE 107.

1. The robbers blamed the leader.
2. A lion was once king of the forest.
3. Charles, the king, was uncle of the leader of the cavalry.
4. Romulus killed his brother.
5. The Gauls had great forces both of cavalry and of
   infantry.
6. It is the voice, not of a man, but of a god.
7. The Romans freed their country from kings and elected
   consuls.
8. Roman soldiers used to dedicate altars to the sun.
9. In London there is a statue of Boadicea, leader of the
   Iceni.
10. Many Christians used to fight against lions at Rome.

EXERCISE 108.

Both men and flocks were in great danger, because a lion
used to wander through the fields. Hercules obeyed King
Eurystheus at once and without delay approached the lion's
lair, because he feared not even lions: so great was the courage
of Hercules. Soon the inhabitants cried out with a loud voice
and praised Hercules, because the lion was now lying dead.
Then they no longer feared danger, but again began to look
after their flocks in the fields. The victory of Hercules, however,
did not please the King of the Argives.

Derivation Test

(*a*) 1. Appāreō.   3. Mīles.   5. Dēmonstrō.
     2. Rex.   4. Hērōs.   6. Sōl.

(*b*) 1. Vocal.   3. Devour.   5. Ducal.
     2. Leonine.   4. Vestige.   6. Frustrate.

Chapter 20

1st and 2nd Conjugations : Future Perfect and Pluperfect Indicative Active ; Future Perfect and Pluperfect Indicative of **sum**

Future Perfect

S. amāverō, *I shall*	monuerō, *I shall*	fuerō, *I shall have*
amāveris *have*	monueris *have*	fueris *been.*
amāverit *loved.*	monuerit *advised.*	fuerit
Pl. amāverimus	monuerimus	fuerimus
amāveritis	monueritis	fueritis
amāverint	monuerint	fuerint

The Future Perfect is naturally used for an action which will have been completed by some time in the Future :

Crās Rōmānōs superāveritis.
Tomorrow you will have overcome the Romans.

The Romans were very precise in their use of Tenses, and in the following example would use the Future Perfect where in English we loosely use the Perfect :

Ubi Rōmānōs superāveritis, laetī eritis.
When you have overcome the Romans, you will be glad.

Often, too, in English we use a Present Tense after *if* and *when*, but the Romans are more correct and use a Future Perfect, if that is the Tense which precisely represents the time of the action :

Sī bellum parāveris, pācem servābis.
If you prepare war, you will preserve peace.

Ubi Rōmam intrāveris, multa templa vidēbis.
When you enter Rome, you will see many temples.

The *preparing* and the *entering* will have to be completed before the *preserving* and the *seeing*.

EXERCISE 109.

(a) 1. Cras patriam vestram a Romanis liberaveritis.
2. Si consul ita imperaverit, adero.
3. Ubi patriam liberaveritis, amici vestri erunt tuti.
4. Longa fuerit via peditibus nostris.
5. Mox oppidum novum aedificaverimus.
6. Dux milites non frustra exercuerit.

(b) 1. Soon you (s.) will have climbed the slope.
2. When you (pl.) have routed the Persians, Greece will be free.
3. Tomorrow we shall have approached the coast of Britain.
4. Give the book to the new master, when he enters.
5. Unless they hurry, the boys will not see the show.
6. Great will have been your (pl.) victory.

Pluperfect

S. amāveram, *I had*	monueram, *I had*	fueram, *I had been.*
amāverās *loved.*	monuerās *advised.*	fuerās
amāverat	monuerat	fuerat
Pl. amāverāmus	monuerāmus	fuerāmus
amāverātis	monuerātis	fuerātis
amāverant	monuerant	fuerant

The Pluperfect is used in Latin as the corresponding tense in English is used:

Herculēs rīdēbat, quod leōnem superāverat.
Hercules was smiling, because he had overcome the lion.

EXERCISE 110.

1. Incolae vestigia leonis Herculi iam monstraverant.
2. Calgacus, quod Romani Caledoniam penetraverant, milites convocavit.
3. Nonne dux viam equitibus monstraverat?

4. Leo incolas saepe terruerat.
5. Agricola multos Britannos conciliaverat, quod erat vir bonus et iustus.
6. Cacus cenam bonam speraverat.
7. Diu fuerant reges Romae.
8. Pyrrhus elephantos ad bellum exercuerat.
9. Cur milites de periculo non monueras?
10. Quod Romulus non apparuerat, Romani diu tacuerant.

EXERCISE 111.

ANDROCLUS AND THE LION: (1) THE LION IN THE CIRCUS

The emperor in whose reign this incident is said to have taken place, was Claudius, A.D. 41-54.

In Circo Maximo Caesar pugnam populo dabat. Inter multas feras apparuerat leo magnus et saevus; iam voce dira populum terruerat. Intraverat ad pugnam inter ceteros servos Androclus; leo tamen, ubi hominem videt, placidus[1] appropinquat. Tum caudam blando modo movet palmasque et membra hominis, iam propter terrorem prope mortui, lingua demulcet. Subito Androclus animum reciperat, leonem rursus spectat; amicum, non periculum, videt.

[1] An Adjective is often used in Latin where in English we use an Adverb or an Adverbial phrase, e.g. **appropinquant laetī,** *they approach joyfully* or *with joy*.

EXERCISE 112.

1. The leader of the cavalry had not reconnoitred the wood.
2. The Britons had already burned St. Albans and Colchester.
3. Antoninus built a rampart because the barbarians had often attacked the Romans.
4. Before the consuls there had been kings.
5. Agricola's victories had not always been welcome to Domitian.
6. Tarquinius Priscus had built the Circus at Rome.
7. Romulus had not yet reviewed the troops.

8. Xerxes had trained many soldiers for the war.
9. The Britons had not had helmets.
10. Suetonius had hurried to London with cavalry.

EXERCISE 113.

Many men had entered the Circus and were sitting in the sun. They had already watched many fights and were now afraid, because a big fierce lion was filling the Circus with his terrible voice. Then a wretched slave entered with the others. The lion, when he sees Androclus, does not start a fight, but wags his tail and comes up to the man gently; then he licks Androclus with his tongue. Always before the lions had attacked and devoured the slaves. Never before had so great a wonder appeared before the eyes of the people.

Derivation Test

1. **Spectāculum.**   2. **Circus.**   3. **Placidus.**   4. **Membrum.**
5. **Modus.**

Chapter 21

3rd Declension : Nouns with Consonant Stems, neuter

Neuter Nouns with Consonant Stems of the 3rd Declension have the same endings as 3rd Decl. masc. and fem. Nouns with Consonant Stems, except that the Nom., Voc., and Acc. sing. have the same form, and these three Cases end in -a in the plur.

Stem	capit- *head* (n.)	oper- *work* (n.)	carmin- *song,poem*(n.)
Sing.			
Nom.	caput	opus	carmen
Voc.	caput	opus	carmen
Acc.	caput	opus	carmen
Gen.	capitis	operis	carminis
Dat.	capitī	operī	carminī
Abl.	capite	opere	carmine
Plur.			
Nom.	capita	opera	carmina
Voc.	capita	opera	carmina
Acc.	capita	opera	carmina
Gen.	capitum	operum	carminum
Dat.	capitibus	operibus	carminibus
Abl.	capitibus	operibus	carminibus

Like the above are declined the following neuter Nouns: onus, oneris, *burden*; corpus, corporis, *body*; vulnus, vulneris, *wound*; crūs, crūris, *leg*; nōmen, nōminis, *name*; flūmen, flūminis, *river*; aēs aēris, *copper, bronze*.

EXERCISE 114.

1. Opus militum duci placebat.
2. Puella capita florum desecabat.

3. Ignorasne nomen floris?
4. Magister pueros carmen novum docebit.
5. Nostri multa vulnera in proelio sustinuerant.
6. Multi pueri corpora in campo hodie exercebant.
7. Erant leoni crura valida.
8. Onera magna pedites in via tardant.
9. Carmina Homeri sunt magnum opus.
10. Dux milites nomine appellabat et ad opus vocabat.

EXERCISE 115.

ANDROCLUS AND THE LION:
(2) ANDROCLUS BEGINS HIS STORY

Miraculum clamores populi statim excitavit et Caesar
Androclum vocavit; Androclum causam miraculi rogavit.
'Leones' inquit, 'semper homines oppugnant et corpora de-
vorant. Cur leo hodie ne oppugnavit quidem?' Androclus
respondet: 'Dominus meus provinciam Africam obtinebat;
vir tamen iniustus erat corpusque meum verberibus coti-
dianis mulcabat. Propter vulnera iratus, in locum desertum
festinavi; ibi, quod ob solem meridianum aegrotabam, antrum
intravi remotum. Mox et leo intravit; murmuribus clamabat
magnis, quod in pede vulnus habebat. Primo ob periculum
pavebam; deinde tamen leo placidus appropinquabat; pedem
levavit et, ut apparebat, auxilium meum oravit.'

EXERCISE 116.

1. There are many rivers in Gaul.
2. The name of the river[1] is the Rhone.
3. The Roman people endured many burdens under the
   kings.
4. The boys and girls were singing songs in the school.
5. The general called the soldiers from their work
6. The Britons used to import copper.
7. The Romans exercised their bodies on the Campus
   Martius.

[1] The *river* should be put into the Dative of the Possessor.

8. Weary because of their wounds, our men lay in the wood.
9. The lion had a large head.
10. Many flowers have long names.

EXERCISE 117.

At once the people began to shout, and Caesar called the slave to his throne. 'Why', said he, 'are you still unhurt?' Then Androclus told Caesar a wonderful story. ' I once lived in Africa; my master used to beat my back with many lashes; therefore, tired with my wounds, I hurried from my master's house into the desert. There, on account of the mid-day sun, I went into a cave. Soon a lion also entered the cave. At first I was afraid of the lion's loud roars; then the lion gently came near and lifted up a blood-stained foot.'

Derivation Test

(*a*) 1. Caput.
2. Opus.
3. Nōmen.
4. Flōs.
5. Tardō.
6. Ūnus.

(*b*) 1. Corporal.
2. Vulnerable.
3. Exonerate.
4. Reverberate.
5. Longitude.
6. Meridian.

Chapter 22

Personal Pronouns: 1st and 2nd Persons

A Personal **Pronoun** is a word put in the place of a Noun (**prō nōmine**), to point to a Person or thing, without giving a name: *I, you* (s.), *he, she, it, we, you* (pl.), *they*.

We have seen already that in Latin these Personal Pronouns can be expressed by the ending of the Verb, e.g. of **amō**, *I love*, but the Verb-ending does not contain any Pronoun except as Subject of the Verb, i.e. in the Nominative. Pronouns, however, can be expressed separately from the Verb in Latin, and their Declension contains the Nominative as well as other Cases.

		1st Person		2nd Person
Sing.				
Nom.	ego,	*I.*	tū,	*you* (also Voc.).
Acc.	mē,	*me.*	tē,	*you.*
Gen.	meī,	*of me.*	tuī,	*of you.*
Dat.	mihi,	*to* or *for me.*	tibi,	*to* or *for you.*
Abl.	mē,	*me.*	tē,	*you.*
Plur.				
Nom.	nōs,	*we.*	vōs,	*you* (also Voc.).
Acc.	nōs,	*us.*	vōs,	*you.*
Gen.	nostrī or	*of us.*	vestrī or	*of you.*
	nostrum,		vestrum,	
Dat.	nōbīs,	*to* or *for us.*	vōbīs,	*to* or *for you.*
Abl.	nōbīs,	*us.*	vōbīs,	*you.*

Dominus meus mē mulcābat.
My master used to beat me.

Rōmānī vōs nōn superābunt.
The Romans will not conquer you.

A Pronoun is not expressed separately in the Nom. Case as the Subject of a Verb, except to call special attention to the Subject, or for the sake of contrast between two Persons:

> **Tūne librum cēlāvistī?**
> *Have you hidden the book?* (with the emphasis on *you*)

> **Tū es nauta, ego sum mīles.**
> *You are a sailor, I am a soldier.* (contrast)

Nostrum, vestrum are used after Numbers and words expressing a Part:

> **Ūnus vestrum abest.**
> *One of you is not here.*

> **Paucī nostrum semper sunt bonī.**
> *Few of us are always good.*

For other purposes **nostrī, vestrī** are used:

> **Amor vestrī rēgem movēbit.**
> *Love of you* (or *for you*) *will influence the king.*

When **cum,** *with,* is used with the Abl. sing. or Abl. plur. of ego or tū, it is written after the Pronoun, to form one word— **mēcum, tēcum, nōbīscum, vōbīscum.**

Composite Subject of different Persons

If a Verb has more than one Subject, and the Subjects are different in Person, then the Verb (*a*) will be in the Plural, (*b*) will agree with the 1st Person rather than the 2nd, and with the 2nd rather than the 3rd:

> **Ego et leō antrum intrāverāmus.**
> *The lion and I had entered the cave.*

There is a point about order to notice here: in Latin the First Person comes before any other Person.

Reflexive Pronouns of 1st and 2nd Persons

The Pronouns of the 1st and 2nd Persons are also used, in the Oblique Cases (Acc., Gen., Dat., and Abl.), as **Reflexives**, e.g. **mē culpō**, *I blame myself*. *Reflexive* (from the Verb **reflectō**) means *bending back*, and Reflexive Pronouns *bend back* towards the Subject: they are used when the person they refer to is the same person as the Subject of their sentence.

So: **Nōn vōbīs labōrātis.**

> *You are not working for yourselves* (the Subject being *you*, in the Verb).

Possessive Pronouns of 1st and 2nd Persons

These are used as Adjectives and have been met already— **meus, tuus, noster, vester.** They should be used to make clear *who* possesses something; otherwise they are often left out:

> **Cum sorōre meā ambulābat.**
> *He was walking with my sister.*

But:

> **Cum sorōre ambulābam.**
> *I was walking with my sister.*

EXERCISE 118.

1. Demonstra mihi virtutem tuam, o Hercules.
2. Et flores et vinum vobis dabimus.
3. Vos Romani estis; ego sum Britannus.
4. Num tu et amici desperatis?
5. Cur te leo non devoravit? Cur tecum non certavit?
6. Multi nostrum viam ignorabant.
7. Tuumne librum dextra tenes?
8. Non modo nobis, sed etiam liberis laboramus.
9. Epistolam a te exspectamus.
10. Sunt mihi multi pedites, pauci equites.

EXERCISE 119.

ANDROCLUS AND THE LION:
(3) THE END OF THE STORY

In leonis pede spina magna haerebat; statim pedem a spina liberavi et cruorem siccavi. Tum leo in bracchiis meis pedem locavit et dormitavit. Diu in antro una habitabamus ego et leo; membra ferarum ad me portabat cibumque praebebat. Hominum tamen amicitiam desideravi; per locum igitur desertum procul ab antro ambulo; tandem milites Romani me vident et ad dominum ex Africa Romam transportant. Hic dominus me damnavit; hodie me bestiis dabat. Leonem quoque, ut apparet, milites Romam transportaverunt; leo propter beneficium et medicinam gratiam mihi habet. Inde Caesar 'A poena', inquit, 'laetus te libero et tibi do leonem.' Postea Androclus et leo circum tabernas errabant: populus Androclo aes dabat, leonem floribus coronabat. Multi exclamabant, 'Spectate leonem, hospitem hominis, et hominem, medicum leonis.'

EXERCISE 120.
1. The master will give you (s.) a new book.
2. Were you (s.) waiting for a letter from me?
3. Sometimes the Romans used to establish friendship with us.
4. You are soldiers; I am a farmer.
5. You (s.) are tiring yourself with much work.
6. At last you (pl.) have consuls instead of kings.
7. I will walk in your garden with my friends.
8. Because of his envy of you, Caesar recalls you to Rome.
9. The deserter's plan does not please me.
10. Our men will always fight for your country.

EXERCISE 121
'The lion felt grateful for my good service and lived with me in the cave; he used to kill wild beasts and provide food for me; I used to roast my food with the mid-day sun. At length, because I yearned for the voices of men, I again wandered into

the desert. I was not, however, free for long. Today you see me again a slave, and a wretched man. In the Circus the lion recognised a friend after many years because of my kindness.' Because the people so demanded, Caesar set Androclus free. Afterwards the lion used to walk through the streets with his doctor.

Derivation Test

(*a*) 1. **Ego.**   2. **Virtūs.**   3. **Exclāmō.**   4. **Medicīna.**

(*b*) 1. Gratitude.   2. Beast.   3. Spine.   4. Desiccated.

Chapter 23

Demonstrative Pronoun : **is, ea, id,** and its use as a Pronoun of the 3rd Person

---

Latin has no Personal Pronoun corresponding to *he, she, it, they*. Instead it uses a Demonstrative Pronoun, i.e. a Pronoun which *points out* (**dēmonstrat**) a person or thing. The one which is most commonly used for this purpose is **is, ea, id.**

Examples of its uses are given after the Declension. There is no Vocative.

Sing.	M.	F.	N.	*Plur.*	M.	F.	N.
Nom.	is	ea	id		eī	eae	ea
Acc.	eum	eam	id		eōs	eās	ea
Gen.	ēius	ēius	ēius		eōrum	eārum	eōrum
Dat.	eī	eī	eī		eīs	eīs	eīs
Abl.	eō	eā	eō		eīs	eīs	eīs

Ubi leō antrum intrāvit, Androclus eum cūrāvit.
When the lion came into the cave, Androclus looked after him.

Eam salūtō, *I greet her.*   **Id nōs dēlectat,** *it delights us.*

Note. In translating from English into Latin, we must remember that *it* may refer to something that is masc. or fem. in Latin, in which case we must use the correct gender; in the same way care must be taken in translating *they* and *them:*

They dedicated an altar to the sun, because they worshipped it.

Āram sōlī consecrāvērunt, quod eum adōrābant.

Ēius, etc., used to express Possession

The Gen. sing. of **is, ea, id,** when used as a Pronoun, is used

118

to express *his*, *her*, *its*, and the Gen. plur. to express *their*, when *his*, *her*, etc., do not refer to the Subject of the sentence:

Latīnus Aenēae et sociīs ēius agrum praebuit.
Latinus provided land for Aeneas and his friends.

Rōmulus nōn iam oculīs eōrum appārēbat.
Romulus no longer appeared to their eyes.

Is, ea, id, used as an Adjective

Is, ea, id, is also used as a Demonstrative Adjective with a Noun, meaning *this* or *that* (without any emphasis) person or thing:

Mox Rōmam vidēbitis: id oppidum est caput Italiae.
Soon you will see Rome: that town is the capital of Italy.

That of, those of

In English we can say *look after your own books and those of your friend* or *look after your own books and your friend's*. The second way is the Latin way: no Pronoun for *that* or *those* is used before a Genitive. The Latin for this sentence is therefore:

Cūrā librōs tuōs et amīcī.

EXERCISE 122.

1. Ad Rhenum appropinquamus: id flumen est latum.
2. Consilium eius Romanis non placuit.
3. Tum Tarquinius Priscus regnavit: is rex cloacas Romae aedificavit.
4. Quod libri me delectant, eos curo.
5. Arma eorum sunt antiqua.
6. Non nostras copias sed Gallorum spectas.
7. Caesar auxilium eorum exspectabat.
8. Leo pedem levabat, quod spina in eo erat.

9. Si patriam amatis, pro ea pugnabitis.
10. Rex Aeneam iuvat et ei dat filiam.

EXERCISE 123.

ALEXANDER'S HORSE

Alexander the Great (356-323 B.C.), *King of Macedonia, fought against the Indians in* 327 B.C.

Equus erat Alexandro, nomine Bucephalas. Servi eum ad proelium saepe ornaverant et armaverant; neminem tamen nisi regem in tergo tolerabat. In bello Indico Alexander in eo insidebat; forte tamen, quod pericula non satis providebat, in copias Indorum incautus properavit. Undique Indi tela in regem iactabant; multa eorum in equi latere haerebant. Moribundus tandem equus regem e periculo extra tela reportat; ubi dominum adhuc salvum videt, exspirat. Alexander post victoriam eius belli oppidum in eo loco aedificavit idque ob equi honorem nomine eius appellavit.

The name he gave the town was Bucephalos.

EXERCISE 124.
1. Cacus was an inhabitant of that place.
2. The cows entered his cave backwards.
3. Their lowing[1] rouses Hercules.
4. Hercules entered the cave and killed him.
5. The Britons worshipped not only native gods, but also those of the Romans.
6. Even women were fighting; the Druids armed them with torches.
7. The people greet Androclus and give him money.
8. The lion used to wander through the streets with him.
9. I am staying in Chester: in this town there was once a camp.
10. Eurystheus was preparing Hercules's destruction rather than the lion's.

[1] Use vox.

EXERCISE 125.

Alexander, King of Macedonia, conquered many lands and even penetrated India. He had a horse, by name Bucephalas; this horse obeyed no one except[1] Alexander. Once Alexander was fighting against the Indians and hurried into danger incautiously; the horse, nearly dead on account of many wounds, carried him safe from the battle to the camp of the Macedonians. Alexander was grateful to him and in return for his good service called a new town by his name.

[1] Use **nisi**, as in Ex. 123, with same case after it as before it.

Derivation Test

(*a*) 1. **Tolerō.** 2. **Latus.** 3. **Appellō.** 4. **Salvus.**

(*b*) 1. Lever. 2. Honourable. 3. Ornament. 4. Adhere.

Chapter 24

Reflexive Pronouns of 3rd Person

Sing. and Plur., all genders.

Acc.	sē or sēsē,	*himself, herself, itself, themselves.*
Gen.	suī,	*of himself,* etc.
Dat.	sibi,	*to* or *for himself,* etc.
Abl.	sē or sēsē,	*himself,* etc.

This Pronoun is used to express *himself, herself, itself, themselves,* when the person they refer to is the **same** person as the Subject of their sentence:

> **Mīlitēs ad proelium sē parābant** (sē and **mīlitēs** being the same persons).
> *The soldiers were getting themselves ready for battle.*

> **Agricolà nōn modo sibi, sed etiam līberīs labōrat.**
> *The farmer works not only for himself, but also for his children.*

When **cum,** *with,* is used with the Abl. of sē, it is written **sēcum.**

Possessive Pronoun of *sē*

This is **suus, sua, suum,** *his* (*own*), *her* (*own*), *its* (*own*), *their* (*own*); it is used as an Adjective and, like sē, it is Reflexive, i.e. it is only used when the *his, her,* etc., refers to the Subject of the sentence.

It is declined like **bonus,** except that it has no Vocative.

Suus is an emphatic Pronoun and is only used when *his, her,* etc., is stressed, or when it would otherwise be doubtful *who* possesses something:

> **Cācus nōn suās, sed Herculis vaccās cēlāvit.**
> *Cacus hid not his own cows, but those of Hercules.*

122

But, **fīlium videt**, *he sees his son*, no Possessive Adjective being needed.

Suī is often used Reflexively as a plur. masc. Noun for *his, her, their, friends, soldiers, relations*, etc.:

> **Caesar suōs confirmāvit.**
> *Caesar encouraged his men.*

EXERCISE 126.

1. Boni non se laudant.
2. Latrones se in amphoris celaverunt.
3. Troiani domicilium sibi orabant.
4. Romani non in sua patria pugnant.
5. Interdum in bello milites agros suos vastant.
6. Caesar multos equites in Britanniam secum transportavit.
7. Britanni villas Verulamii sibi aedificaverunt.
8. Dux suos in castra revocaverat.
9. Non sua virtute is homo regnum comparavit.
10. Propter amorem sui non multis placet.

EXERCISE 127.

GEESE SAVE THE CAPITOL

Gauls from the north of Italy attacked and captured Rome in 390 B.C. They were unable, however, to take the citadel, called the Capitol.

Romae Capitolium in magno periculo fuit. Forte enim Galli vestigium humanum in clivo notaverant. Noctu igitur unus ex eis[1] viam temptat. Inde multi pone eum appropinquabant; arma proximis dabant, et, ubi locus erat iniquus, comites invicem sublevabant et tractabant; propter silentium Capitolii custodes non excitaverunt. Anseres tamen vigilabant; quod anseres Iunoni erant sacri, Romani in magna inopia cibi ab eis abstinuerant. Anseres Romanos et Capitolium

---

[1] **ex** or **ē** with Abl. is often used, instead of a Gen., after Numerals and words expressing Number.

conservaverunt; Manlium[1] enim magno clangore excitaverunt. Is suos ad arma vocat, et, dum reliqui trepidant, primum Gallorum de saxo praecipitat; is Gallus proximos sibi ruina sua deturbat.

[1] Manlius had held the office of consul, but was later put to death for aiming at too much power.

EXERCISE 128.

1. Foolish men praise themselves.
2. The girls were exercising themselves.
3. The soldiers carry nothing with them except swords.
4. The farmer is building a cottage for himself.
5. The leader had wandered from his men.
6. He was not carrying his own sword, but his friend's.
7. The boys invited their sisters.
8. The boys have not their own books.
9. Alexander called many towns by his own name.
10. The consul is showing the plan to his friends.

EXERCISE 129.

The Gauls had burnt Rome; nothing was left except the Capitol. There were many men there, but no one was awake, because they did not fear danger: even the guards were giving themselves to sleep. The Gauls climbed the high rock, but by chance roused the geese; these geese were sacred to Juno and on account of this the Romans had spared them. The geese awoke Manlius, Manlius awoke his men. The first Gaul was now standing on the Capitol, but Manlius hurled him headlong on to[1] those[2] next to him.

[1] Use in with Acc.
[2] *those* is not to be translated; see Ex. 127, last sentence.

Derivation Test

1. Temptation. 2. Alexandria. 3. Excitement. 4. Trepidation.

Chapter 25

3rd Declension : Nouns with I- Stems, masculine and feminine

Most of the Nouns with Consonant Stems which have been learnt so far have one more syllable in the Gen. sing. than in the Nom. sing. e.g. **rex, rēgis,** *king.* Exceptions were **pater, māter, frāter.**

There is a large number of 3rd Decl. masc. and fem. Nouns, which have an equal number of syllables in the Nom. and Gen. sing. Their Stem ends in **i-** and their Gen. plur. ends in **-ium.**

Stem	hosti- enemy (c.).	imbri- shower (m.).	nūbi- cloud (f.).
Sing.			
Nom.	hostis	imber	nūbēs
Voc.	hostis	imber	nūbēs
Acc.	hostem	imbrem	nūbem
Gen.	hostis	imbris	nūbis
Dat.	hostī	imbrī	nūbī
Abl.	hoste	imbre	nūbe
Plur.			
Nom.	hostēs	imbrēs	nūbēs
Voc.	hostēs	imbrēs	nūbēs
Acc.	hostēs (or -īs)	imbrēs (or -īs)	nūbēs (or -īs)
Gen.	hostium	imbrium	nūbium
Dat.	hostibus	imbribus	nūbibus
Abl.	hostibus	imbribus	nūbibus

Hostis means an *enemy of one's country* as opposed to **inimīcus,** a *private enemy*; **hostis** is usually found in the plur.

Like **hostis** are declined **cīvis** (c.), *citizen*; **nāvis** (f.), *ship*; **ignis** (m.), *fire* (Abl. usually **ignī**). So also **iuvenis** (c.), *young person*, and **canis** (c.), *dog*, except that they form their Gen. plur. in **-um.**

Like **imber** is declined **linter** (f.), *boat.*
Like **nūbēs** are declined **clādēs** (f.), *disaster* ; **rūpēs** (f.), *rock.*

3rd Conjugation: Present Indicative Active

Most Verbs of the 3rd Conjugation have a Stem which ends
in a Consonant. Below is the Present Tense of **reg-ō,** *I rule* : it is
conjugated exactly like the Future Tense of **sum (erō)** :

Sing.	reg-o,	*I rule.*
	reg-is,	*you rule,* etc.
	reg-it	
Plur.	reg-imus	
	reg-itis	
	reg-unt	

So also **dūcō,** *I lead* ; **trahō,** *I drag* ; **discēdō,** *I depart* ; **dēdō,** *I
give up* ; **mittō,** *I send* ; **vincō,** *I conquer.*

EXERCISE 130.

1. Boudicca Icenos regit.
2. Cur discedunt hostes?
3. Calgacus copias hostium ducit.
4. Fabricius perfugam ad hostes mittit.
5. Imber magnus ignem vincit.
6. Iuvenes non navigant, sed lintrem trahunt.
7. Tanta clades cives Romanos non vincit.
8. Erant hostibus multae naves.
9. Multitudo hostium igni et ferro terram vastabat.
10. Ludi iuvenum patres delectant.

EXERCISE 131.

THE ROMANS AND THE SABINES:
(1) THE CAPTURE OF THE BRIDES

*Owing to a shortage of women the Romans, during the reign
of Romulus, obtain wives by a trick from their neighbours, the
Sabines.*

Non erant Romae satis multae mulieres. Cives igitur multos finitimos ad ludos invitaverunt. Sabinorum multitudo una cum liberis et coniugibus Romam intrat. Dum spectaculo se dedunt, subito iuvenes Romani virgines Sabinas a parentibus trahunt; parentes earum sine mora maesti e finibus Romanis discedunt. Romulus animos virginum confirmabat. 'Romae adestis,' inquit, 'quod parentes vestri conubium finitimis recusabant. Hic fortunam nostram vobiscum communicabimus.' Tum viri Sabinas amore vincunt et iram earum mitigant.

EXERCISE 132.

1. Gyges now rules the Lydians.
2. Caesar sends many ships to Britain.
3. The Gauls destroy the town with fire and depart.
4. The Gauls aroused not even the dogs.
5. The fire penetrated even the clouds.
6. Many of the enemy are giving themselves up.
7. Caesar is leading his men against the enemy.
8. Cacus drags the cows into the cave.
9. The Roman citizens drive out the kings.
10. The Romans had few ships, the enemy had many.

EXERCISE 133.

Romulus sends messengers to the Sabines and invites them to the games. Many Sabines, guests of the Roman citizens, enter the town and praise the walls and buildings. Then they give themselves up to the show. Suddenly Roman young men run from the games to the place where the Sabines are sitting. At once they drag the maidens from the arms of their parents and lead them away. The parents call upon[1] the gods, because the Romans have violated hospitality.

[1] invocō (with Acc.).

Derivation Test

(*a*) 1. **Nāvis.**   2. **Canis.**   3. **Ignis.**   4. **Commūnicō.**

(*b*) 1. **Hostile.**   2. Civic.   3. Regent.   4. Juvenile.

Chapter 26

3rd Declension: Nouns with I- Stems, neuter

Neuter Nouns with I- Stems of the 3rd Declension end in -e, -l, or -r. The i- of the Stem is kept throughout, after the first three Cases of the Sing.: it should be noticed particularly that the Abl. sing. ends in -ī.

Stem	cubīli- *couch* (n.).	animāli- *animal* (n.).	calcāri- *spur* (n.).
Sing.			
Nom.	cubīle	animal	calcar
Voc.	cubīle	animal	calcar
Acc.	cubīle	animal	calcar
Gen.	cubīlis	animālis	calcāris
Dat.	cubīlī	animālī	calcārī
Abl.	cubīlī	animālī	calcārī
Plur.			
Nom.	cubīlia	animālia	calcāria
Voc.	cubīlia	animālia	calcāria
Acc.	cubīlia	animālia	calcāria
Gen.	cubīlium	animālium	calcārium
Dat.	cubīlibus	animālibus	calcāribus
Abl.	cubīlibus	animālibus	calcāribus

Like **cubīle** are declined: **mare**, *sea* (Gen. pl. not in use); **conclāve**, *room*.

Like **animal** is declined: **vectīgal**, *tax*.

Note. **Terrā marīque**, *by land and sea*.

3rd Declension: masc. and fem. Nouns of one syllable, ending with two Consonants, etc.

Most Nouns of this type originally had two syllables in the Nom., and belong really to the **hostis** type. Nouns ending in **-tās** are also declined in the same way.

Stem	urbi- *city* (f.).	ponti- *bridge* (m.).	cīvitāti- *state* (f.).
Sing.			
Nom.	urbs	pons	cīvitās
Voc.	urbs	pons	cīvitās
Acc.	urbem	pontem	cīvitātem
Gen.	urbis	pontis	cīvitātis
Dat.	urbī	pontī	cīvitātī
Abl.	urbe	ponte	cīvitāte
Plur.			
Nom.	urbēs	pontēs	cīvitātēs
Voc.	urbēs	pontēs	cīvitātēs
Acc.	urbēs (or -īs)	pontēs (or -īs)	cīvitātēs (or -īs)
Gen.	urbium	pontium	cīvitātium
Dat.	urbibus	pontibus	cīvitātibus
Abl.	urbibus	pontibus	cīvitātibus

So also: **arx, arcis** (f.), *citadel*; **mons, montis** (m.), *mountain*; **fons, fontis** (m.), *fountain*; **frons, frontis** (f.), *forehead, front*. **Nox, noctis** (f.), *night* is declined in the same way.

3rd Conjugation: Future and Imperfect Indicative Active

	Future Tense	Imperfect Tense
Sing.	reg-am, *I shall rule.*	reg-ēbam, *I was ruling.*
	reg-ēs	reg-ēbās
	reg-et	reg-ēbat
Plur.	reg-ēmus	reg-ēbāmus
	reg-ētis	reg-ēbātis
	reg-ent	reg-ēbant

Some more 3rd Conjugation Verbs: **scrībō**, *I write*; **ascendō**, *I climb*; **gerō**, *I carry, wage*; **rumpō**, *I break*; **petō**, *I seek, attack, make for*.

Note. **Scrībō ad** with Acc., *I write to* someone.

Exercise 134.

1. Pueri aegri in cubilibus iacent.
2. Dux equum calcaribus regebat.

3. Multa animalia sunt hominum amici.
4. Hostes pontem non rumpent.
5. Romani vectigal ab urbibus petebant.
6. Montem ante noctem non ascendemus.
7. Caesar bellum contra civitates Gallicas gerebat.
8. Pompeius mare a praedonibus liberavit.
9. Urbem a fronte non oppugnabimus.
10. Cicero multas epistolas ad amicos scribebat.

EXERCISE 135.

THE ROMANS AND THE SABINES:
(2) THE SABINES' REVENGE

Tarpeius Romanae arci praeerat. Forte filia eius aquam e fonte extra arcem petebat. Tatius, dux Sabinorum, ad eam appropinquat et aurum promittit; propter aurum ea hostes admittit in urbem. Sabini, si fabulae credimus, in bracchiis laevis aureas armillas magni ponderis habebant. Ea pro beneficio suo ornamentum bracchiorum laevorum postulaverat; hostes tamen scuta, non armillas, in eam congerunt. Ita eam opprimunt et necant.

The place where this happened became known as the Tarpeian Rock, and traitors were executed there.

EXERCISE 136.

1. Many states send taxes to Rome.
2. We were waging war by land and sea.
3. We will seek safety in the mountains.
4. The animals were waiting for the night in their lairs.
5. Our men will break a way through the enemy.
6. Were you (s.) making for the city of Rome?
7. I will write a letter to him tomorrow.
8. There was a beautiful fountain in the city.
9. Many men were climbing the high mountain.
10. The infantry began to break down their own bridge.

EXERCISE 137.

Soon the Sabines entered the city by a trick. Owing to a scarcity of water the Romans sought it outside the citadel.

Tarpeius therefore used to send his daughter to the fountain. The leader of the Sabines waits for her there and promises her gold. In return for that reward she lets the soldiers into the city. She had demanded, as the story relates, the decoration of their left arms. When, however, they enter, they heap their shields upon[1] her instead of gold.

[1] in with Acc.

Derivation Test

(a) 1. **Urbs.**   2. **Fons.**   3. **Crēdō.**
     4. **Mare.**   5. **Pons.**   6. **Nox.**

(b) 1. Frontal.   2. Ascent.   3. Petition.
     4. Inscribe.   5. Ponderous.   6. Admittance.

3rd Conjugation: Imperative Active

The 2nd pers. sing. of the Imperative Active of **regō**, is **rege**, and the 2nd pers. plur. is **regite**. **Dūcō**, *I lead*, and **dīcō**, *I say*, are irregular and have **dūc** and **dīc** in the sing.

3rd Declension: Locative Case

The Locative Case of the 3rd Declension ends in **-ī** or **-e** in the sing., and in **-ibus** in the plur., e.g. **Carthāginī** or **Carthāgine**, *at Carthage* (**Carthāgō**, f.); **rūrī** or **rūre**, *in the country* (**rūs**, n., *country* as opposed to *town*); **vesperī** or **vespere**, *in the evening* (**vesper**, m.); **Gādibus**, *at Cadiz* (**Gādēs**, f.).

No preposition is ever used with **rūs**. Compare the rule about towns and small islands:

> **Rūre properāmus.**
> *We hurry from the country.*

EXERCISE 138.

1. Scribe epistolam hodie.
2. Manete ruri, o liberi.
3. Rumpite pontem sine mora.
4. Amicitiam bonorum semper pete.

5. Templum Herculis Gadibus erat.
6. Hannibal Carthagine non manet.
7. Duc equites in montem.
8. Aut disce aut discede.

EXERCISE 139.
1. Make for (pl.) the mountains.
2. The Britons are hurrying from the colony into the country.
3. Climb up (pl.) the Capitol by night.
4. Write (s.) a long letter to your father.
5. Break (pl.) a way through the city.
6. The enemy are sailing from Carthage.
7. Go away, boys.
8. Speak (s.) the truth,[1] my friend.

[1] Neuter pl. of **vērus**, *true* : so also **falsa dīcō**, *I tell lies.*

Chapter 27

Adjectives of 3rd Declension with three endings

3rd Declension Adjectives with three different endings for masc., fem., and neut., follow the declension of I- Stem Nouns. The Abl. sing. always ends in -ī; with this exception, the masc. is declined like **imber**; the fem. like **hostis**; the neuter exactly follows **cubīle**.

Stem   **ācri-**, *keen, fierce.*

Sing.	M.	F.	N.
Nom.	ācer	ācris	ācre
Voc.	ācer	ācris	ācre
Acc.	ācrem	ācrem	ācre
Gen.	ācris	ācris	ācris
Dat.	ācrī	ācrī	ācrī
Abl.	ācrī	ācrī	ācrī
Plur.			
Nom.	ācrēs	ācrēs	ācria
Voc.	ācrēs	ācrēs	ācria
Acc.	ācrēs (or -īs)	ācrēs (or -īs)	ācria
Gen.	ācrium	ācrium	ācrium
Dat.	ācribus	ācribus	ācribus
Abl.	ācribus	ācribus	ācribus

So also: **alacer**, *active, eager*; **celeber**, *famous*; **salūber**, *healthy*; **paluster**, *marshy*; **equester**, *of cavalry.*

Celer, celeris, celere, *swift*, keeps **-er** throughout, and has Gen. plur. **celerum.**

4th Conjugation: Present Indicative Active

Verbs of the 4th Conjugation have a Stem which ends in **ī-**. Below is the Present Tense of **audi-ō**, *I hear*: the vowel of the Stem appears throughout.

Sing.	**audi-ō**, *I hear.*
	audī-s, *you hear*, etc.
	audi-t
Plur.	**audī-mus**
	audī-tis
	audi-unt

So also: **impediō**, *I hinder*; **mūniō**, *I fortify, build (road)*; **veniō**, *I come* (**perveniō ad**, *I reach, arrive at*); **inveniō**, *I find*; **aperiō**, *I open.*

Inter sē

Latin uses **inter sē** after a Transitive Verb in the 3rd person plur. to express *each other*; literally it would mean *between themselves* (Reflexive):

Rōmānī et Britannī inter sē pugnābant.
The Romans and Britons were fighting each other.

EXERCISE 140.

1. Londinium est oppidum celebre et salubre.
2. Pueri non sunt alacres hodie.
3. Tarpeia portam arcis aperit.
4. Romani multas vias per Britanniam muniunt.
5. Nostri Britannos equestri proelio vincunt.
6. Subito Galli ad portam Romae perveniunt.
7. Aures canum sunt acres.
8. Manlius consilio celeri suos conservavit.
9. Locus paluster nostros impedit.
10. Dux multa ex captivis invenit.

EXERCISE 141.

THE ROMANS AND THE SABINES:
(3) LOVE PROVES MIGHTIER THAN
THE SWORD

Sabini iam arcem tenebant. Inde Romani et Sabini proelio longo et acri inter se pugnant. Mettius Curtius de arce Sabinos ducit et primo Romanos fugat. Deinde subito Romulus cum globo alacrium iuvenum Mettium repellit. Mettius ex[1] equo pugnabat et in locum palustrem se praecipitavit; in magno erat periculo, quod equus trepidabat. Nunc etiam Sabini a pugna desistunt et exclamant. Et locus et equus Mettium impediunt; voces tamen Sabinorum viro animum addunt. Tandem e palude evadit; Romani tamen in pugna superant.

Tum Sabinae mulieres inter tela incedunt et per copias infestas viam rumpunt; pavor eas non impedit. Hinc patres, hinc viros orant. 'Si vobis', inquiunt, 'conubium nostrum displicet, in nos vertite iras; nos causa belli sumus; potius occumbemus quam sine viris et sine patribus vivemus.' Duces Sabinorum taciti ea verba audiunt; tum pacem cum Romanis confirmant.

[1] The Romans were more exact even in their use of Prepositions; English would use *on*.

EXERCISE 142.

1. The Romans were waging a fierce war.
2. His name was celebrated among the Gauls.
3. Caesar's cavalry do not arrive owing to a storm.
4. We are building a country-house in a healthy place.
5. Caesar is fortifying his camp with a rampart and a ditch.
6. Eager and glad, she invites her friends.
7. Your dog has sharp eyes.
8. The boy is opening the door for the master.
9. Our men were driving back the enemy in a cavalry fight.
10. Gyges finds a ring in the cave.

EXERCISE 143.

For a long time the Romans endured a fierce fight. Mettius Curtius leads the Sabines and shouts out, 'We are conquering our faithless hosts.' Against him Romulus urges on some active young men and drives him into marshy ground. By chance Mettius was then fighting on horseback; he was holding back his horse with difficulty,[1] because the shouts of the Romans

[1] *with difficulty*, **vix** (*scarcely*).

frightened him. The Sabines call Mettius towards them and encourage him. He hears their voices and at last reaches his own men.

Derivation Test

(*a*) 1. Alacer. 2. Equester. 3. Ēvādō.
     4. Inveniō. 5. Addō. 6. Infestus.

(*b*) 1. Repel. 2. Salubrious. 3. Celebrity.
     4. Impediment. 5. Perfidious. 6. Audible.

Chapter 28

Adjectives of 3rd Declension, with two endings

3rd Declension Adjectives with two different endings have one ending which serves for both masc. and fem., and one for neut. They follow the Declension of I- Stem Nouns. One of these Adjectives is declined below; it will be seen that **omnis, omne**, *all*, is declined exactly like **ācer, ācris, ācre**, except that the ending in -is is the ending of the Nom. and Voc. of the masc. as well as of the fem. in the singular.

Stem   **omni-**, *all, every.*

Sing.	M. and F.	N.	*Plur.*	M. and F.	N.
Nom.	omnis	omne		omnēs	omnia
Voc.	omnis	omne		omnēs	omnia
Acc.	omnem	omne		omnēs (or -īs)	omnia
Gen.	omnis	omnis		omnium	omnium
Dat.	omnī	omnī		omnibus	omnibus
Abl.	omnī	omnī		omnibus	omnibus

So also: **fortis**, *brave*; **facilis**, *easy*; **difficilis**, *difficult*; **ūtilis**, *useful*; **turpis**, *disgraceful*; **insignis**, *conspicuous.*

4th Conjugation: Future and Imperfect Indicative Active

	Future Tense	Imperfect Tense
Sing.	**audi-am**, *I shall hear.*	**audi-ēbam**, *I was hearing.*
	audi-ēs	**audi-ēbās**
	audi-et	**audi-ēbat**
Plur.	**audi-ēmus**	**audi-ēbāmus**
	audi-ētis	**audi-ēbātis**
	audi-ent	**audi-ēbant**

Some more 4th Conjug. Verbs: **custōdiō**, *I guard*; **saepiō**, *I enclose*; **sentiō**, *I perceive, feel.*

EXERCISE 144.

1. Opus militum non erat facile.
2. Omnes milites erant in castris.
3. Mox omnia audietis, amici.
4. Consilium perfugae utile, non honestum, erat.
5. Viam facilem tibi aperiemus.
6. Tarpeia hostes turpi proditione admittit.
7. Hostes nos undique saepiunt.
8. Romani arcem non satis custodiebant.
9. Socrates propter sapientiam insignis erat.
10. Pyrrhus inopiam copiarum sentiebat.

EXERCISE 145.

THE BRAVERY OF HORATIUS COCLES (1)

*When Tarquinius Superbus, the last of the kings, was expelled
from Rome in* 510 B.C., *he fled for refuge to Etruria, a country to
the north-west of Rome. Here he asked Lars Porsenna, King of
the Etruscans, to help to restore him to the throne.*

Romani Tarquinium ob violentiam turpem expellunt; inde
is auxilium a Porsenna, rege Etruscorum, petit. Porsenna
Romam cum infestis copiis venit.

Quod hostes aderant, omnes cives in urbem ex agris migra-
bant, urbem saepiebant praesidiis. Omnia tuta habebant
praeter pontem sublicium, ubi via facilis hostibus patebat.
Erat tamen unus vir, ante omnes fortis, nomine Horatius
Cocles; is forte pontem custodiebat. Subito Etrusci Ianicu-
lum[1] occupant et inde ad pontem decurrunt. Horatius suos
videt trepidos et incompositos et eos obsecrat. 'Si pontem',
inquit, 'a tergo relinquetis, hostes viam in Capitolium aperient.
Rumpite pontem omni modo; ego meo uno corpore hostibus
resistam.' Vadit inde in primam partem pontis, inter ceteros
insignis.

[1] The Janiculum was one of the hills of Rome, outside the main
walls and across the Tiber.

EXERCISE 146.

1. Soldiers were guarding the camp by night.

2. Their journey was long and difficult.
3. The cause of the war was disgraceful.
4. The Romans did not conquer all Britain.
5. Will not the animals feel the cold?
6. We are enclosing the camp with a rampart.
7. Copper is useful to men.
8. The queen was conspicuous among her troops.
9. The soldiers were making for Dover: this journey was not easy.
10. We shall soon reach the famous fountain.

EXERCISE 147.

All the citizens were in great danger, because the pile bridge offered an easy way to the Etruscans. By chance, however, Horatius Cocles, a brave man, was guarding the bridge. Because the Romans began to leave their ranks, he warned them. 'Cease from disgraceful flight,' said he; 'break the bridge with steel and fire: I will hinder the forces of the enemy.' Already the Etruscans were arriving at the bridge; nearly all the Romans were making for the city.

Derivation Test

(a) 1. Ūtilis.   2. Fortis.   3. Violentia.   4. Omnis.

(b) 1. Facility.   2. Sentiment.   3. Extraordinary.   4. Relinquish.

Chapter 29

Adjectives of 3rd Declension, with one ending

There are a number of 3rd Declension Adjectives with I-Stems which have the same ending for the Nom. and Voc. sing. for all genders. The most common types end in **-ns** or **-x**.

Stem   **ingenti-,** *huge.*

Sing.	M. and F.	N.	*Plur.* M. and F.	N.
Nom.	ingens	ingens	ingentēs	ingentia
Voc.	ingens	ingens	ingentēs	ingentia
Acc.	ingentem	ingens	ingentēs (or -īs)	ingentia
Gen.	ingentis	ingentis	ingentium	ingentium
Dat.	ingentī	ingentī	ingentibus	ingentibus
Abl.	ingentī	ingentī	ingentibus	ingentibus

Stem   **fēlīci-,** *fortunate.*

Sing.	M. and F.	N.	*Plur.* M. and F.	N.
Nom.	fēlix	fēlix	fēlīcēs	fēlīcia
Voc.	fēlix	fēlix	fēlīcēs	fēlīcia
Acc.	fēlīcem	fēlix	fēlīcēs (or -īs)	fēlīcia
Gen.	fēlīcis	fēlīcis	fēlīcium	fēlīcium
Dat.	fēlīcī	fēlīcī	fēlīcibus	fēlīcibus
Abl.	fēlīcī	fēlīcī	fēlīcibus	fēlīcibus

Like ingens are declined : **sapiens,** *wise* ; **recens,** *fresh.*

Like fēlix are declined : **audax (audāc-),** *daring* ; **ferox (ferōc-),** *fierce, spirited* ; **atrox (atrōc-),** *horrible, cruel.*

3rd and 4th Conjugations: Perfect, Future Perfect, and Pluperfect Indicative Active

The Perfect, Future Perfect, and Pluperfect Tenses of the 3rd and 4th Conjugations are formed by adding the regular endings of these Tenses (as already met in the first two Conjugations) to the Perfect Base.

3rd Conjugation
Perfect Base rex-

	Perfect Tense	Future Perfect Tense	Pluperfect Tense
Sing.	rexī, *I ruled* or	rexerō, *I shall*	rexeram, *I had*
	rexistī *have*	rexeris *have*	rexerās *ruled.*
	rexit *ruled.*	rexerit *ruled.*	rexerat
Plur.	reximus	rexerimus	rexerāmus
	rexistis	rexeritis	rexerātis
	rexērunt	rexerint	rexerant

So also: **intellegō**, *I understand*; **neglegō**, *I neglect*; **tegō**, *I cover*.

4th Conjugation
Perfect Base audīv-

	Perfect Tense	Future Perfect Tense	Pluperfect Tense
Sing.	audīvī, *I heard* or	audīverō, *I shall*	audīveram, *I had*
	audīvistī *have*	audīveris *have*	audīverās *heard.*
	audīvit *heard.*	audīverit *heard.*	audīverat
Plur.	audīvimus	audīverimus	audīverāmus
	audīvistis	audīveritis	audīverātis
	audīvērunt	audīverint	audīverant

So also: **custōdiō**, *I guard*; **impediō**, *I hinder*; **mūniō**, *I fortify*; **dormio**, *I sleep*.

Exercise 148.

1. Latrones praedam ingentem comparaverunt.
2. Mettius voces suorum audivit.
3. Pueri sapientes libros non neglexerunt.
4. Leo, propter vulnus recens defessus, dormivit.
5. Nubes nigra montem texerat.
6. Non omnes imperatores sunt in proelio felices.
7. Tempestas atrox nautas terruit.
8. Interdum audaces este, fortes semper.

9. Non frustra verba magistri intellexeritis.
10. Romani labore ingenti castra muniverant.

EXERCISE 149.

THE BRAVERY OF HORATIUS COCLES (2)

Nemo praeter Larcium et Herminium, viros audaces, cum
Horatio manebat. Cum eis parumper primam periculi procellam sustinuit; interim ceteri pontem rumpebant. Post breve
spatium, quod modo parva pars pontis superest, Horatius
comites ad locum tutum remittit. Inde hostes oculis ferocibus
circumspectat et ad pugnam provocat. Etrusci magno cum
clamore in unum hostem tela fundebant; ea omnia in scuto
haerebant. Horatius obstinatus ingenti corpore hostes ali-
quamdiu impediverat; tum subito omnes fragorem audiverunt;
ceteri pontem labefactaverant. Tum Horatius 'Tiberine pater',
inquit, 'et me et arma flumini tuo felici mando.' Ita cum armis
in Tiberim[1] desilit; quanquam multa tela super eum cadunt,
tutus ad suos tranat.

[1] A few I- Stem Nouns in -is prefer Acc. in -im. Abl. in -i.

EXERCISE 150.

1. Had you (s.) heard his voice before?
2. Bold youths were dragging the maidens from their
   parents.
3. Cacus had fortified the door with huge stones.
4. Wise men are not always fortunate.
5. Boadicea was brave in dangers.
6. Calgacus was leading to war a spirited people.
7. The kings fortified Rome with walls.
8. The soldiers had covered their huge shields with skins.
9. Their memory of the victory was fresh.
10. The geese guarded the Capitol, the dogs slept.

EXERCISE 151.

Larcius and Herminius had neglected danger and were
guarding the bridge together with Horatius. Soon only a
small part of the bridge is left. Horatius therefore sends back

his companions and fights alone. Although many called him back, he neglected their words. The battle was long and cruel, but Horatius, bold in danger, hindered the Etruscans from the bridge. When at last, as he understands from[1] the crash, the bridge no longer offers a way to the enemy, he jumps down into the Tiber.

[1] ex.

Derivation Test

(a) 1. **Recens.**   2. **Dormiō**   3. **Atrox.**
    4. **Spatium.**   5. **Audax.**   6. **Intellegō**

(b) 1. Ferocious.   2. Provoke.   3. Brevity.
    4. Munitions.   5. Negligence.   6. Felicitous.

Chapter 30

4th Declension

The Stem of Nouns of the 4th Declension ends in **-u**. This letter regularly appears in all the Cases, except the Dat. and Abl. plural.

Stem	**gradu-** *step* (m.).	**cornu-** *horn, wing (of army)* (n.).
Sing.		
Nom.	**gradus**	**cornū**
Voc.	**gradus**	**cornū**
Acc.	**gradum**	**cornū**
Gen.	**gradūs**	**cornūs**
Dat.	**graduī**	**cornū**
Abl.	**gradū**	**cornū**
Plur.		
Nom.	**gradūs**	**cornua**
Voc.	**gradūs**	**cornua**
Acc.	**gradūs**	**cornua**
Gen.	**graduum**	**cornuum**
Dat.	**gradibus**	**cornibus**
Abl.	**gradibus**	**cornibus**

Like **gradus** are declined: **exercitus** (m.), *army*; **impetus** (m.), *attack*; **senātus** (m.), *senate*; **manus** (f.), *hand, band (of men)*.

Domus (f.), *house*, can be declined regularly like **gradus**, except that it takes a 2nd Decl. form for the Abl. sing., **domō**; in the sing. are also sometimes found Gen. **domī**, Dat. **domō**, and in the plur., Acc. **domōs**, Gen. **domōrum**.

Like **cornū** is declined: **genū**, *knee*.

The only Locative of a Noun of the 4th Decl. is **domī**, *at home* (the form being borrowed from the 2nd Decl.).

Note. The Acc. and Abl. of **domus** are used without a Preposition, to express *to* and *from home*.

4th Conjugation: Imperative Active

The 2nd pers. sing. of the Imperative Active of **audiō** is **audī**, and the 2nd pers. plur. is **audīte**.

3rd and 4th Conjugations:
Different forms of Perfect Base

A. 3rd Conjugation.

The Present Stem of **regō** is **reg-**. The Perfect Base is formed by adding **-s**, which gives us **regs-**, which the Romans slightly changed to **rex-**. To this are added the regular Perfect Endings, **-ī, -istī, -it**, etc., which are found in all Perfect Tenses.

We saw that **intellegō, neglegō, tegō** exactly followed **regō** in the form of their Perfect Base, **intellex-, neglex-, tex-**.

1. Only a few 3rd Conjug. Verbs exactly follow this type, but in a good many others we can see that an **-s** has been added to the Present Stem, though there may be other alterations as well.

(Compounds have the same form, unless stated otherwise, e.g. **discessī**, *I departed*.)

Present Tense	Perfect Tense	
dīcō	dixī	*I say*
dūcō	duxī	*I lead*
gerō	gessī	*I carry*
scrībō	scripsī	*I write*
trahō	traxī	*I drag*
cēdō	cessī	*I go, yield*
lūdō	lūsī	*I play*
mittō	mīsī	*I send*

2. In this group the Verbs use a Base like that of another Conjugation:

pōnō	posuī	*I place* (like 2nd Conj.)
petō	petīvī	*I seek* (like 4th Conj.)

3. Some Verbs do not change their Present Stem:

ascendō	ascendī	*I climb*
occīdō	occīdī	*I kill*
vertō	vertī	*I turn* (trans.)

K

4. Some Verbs lengthen their Present Stem Vowel, with or without other slight change:

legō	lēgī	*I read*
ēligō (compound of legō)	ēlēgī	*I choose*
rumpō	rūpī	*I break*
vincō	vīcī	*I conquer*

5. Some Verbs repeat one of the Consonants and insert a Vowel:

cadō	cecidī	*I fall*
dēdō	dēdidī	*I give up* (trans.)
prōdō	prōdidī	*I betray*

These Perfect Tenses soon become familiar in Translation and are easily learnt by heart.

B. 4th Conjugation.

All the 4th Conjug. Verbs which have occurred so far follow **audīvī** in forming their Perfect Base, e.g. **impedīv-**, **mūnīv-**, etc., except the following, which use a Base like that of another Conjugation:

aperiō	aperuī	*I open*
saepiō	saepsī	*I enclose*
sentiō	sensī	*I feel*
veniō	vēnī	*I come*

So also compounds: **inveniō** *I find*; **perveniō (ad)**, *I reach*.

EXERCISE 152.

1. Romulus manum ferocium iuvenum duxerat.
2. Comites Horatii discesserunt.
3. Romani pontem ruperunt.
4. Horatius Larcium et Herminium ad ceteros remisit.
5. Multi Galli Capitolium ascenderunt.
6. Custodes adventum eorum non senserant.
7. Primus Gallus in suos cecidit.
8. Dux exercitus equites in dextro cornu posuerat.

9. Senatus populusque Romanus[1] Horatio gratiam habebat.
10. Audi mea verba, Tiberine deus.

[1] Often shortened to S.P.Q.R.

EXERCISE 153.

THE BRAVERY OF A ROMAN GIRL

Since Porsenna was unable to storm the city of Rome owing to the bravery of Horatius, he laid siege to it. The Romans, however, killed many Etruscans by ambush, and Mucius, a secret agent, only failed to kill the king, because he killed his secretary in mistake for him. Porsenna was deeply impressed both by the bravery of Mucius, who thrust his right hand into the fire, when he had ordered him to be burnt to death, and by his statement that there were in Rome three hundred more secret agents like him. At this point the account of the war is continued in the following piece:

Porsenna tandem legatos ad senatum misit. Romani Tarquinios non restituerunt, obsides tamen Porsennae dediderunt; inde Porsenna a Ianiculo exercitum deduxit et ex agro Romano discessit.

Forte Etrusci castra non procul a ripa Tiberis posuerant. Cloelia virgo, una ex obsidibus, dux manus virginum, custodes elusit et inter tela hostium Tiberim tranavit; omnes virgines salvas ad propinquos reduxit. Porsenna, ubi audivit[1], oratores ad senatum iratus misit et Cloeliam obsidem postulavit. Deinde admiratio eum vicit: 'Nisi obsidem', inquit, 'dedideritis, foedus rumpetis; Cloeliam tamen, si eam dedideritis, ad propinquos remittam.' Et Romani et Etrusci foedus conservaverunt. Porsenna enim non modo Cloeliam laudavit, sed etiam ei partem obsidum promisit. Cloelia tamen non virgines, ut rex exspectaverat, sed iuvenes elegit et ita ab hostibus liberavit. Romani tantam virginis virtutem statua equestri honoraverunt; in Sacra Via sedet virgo in equo.

[1] ubi, *when*, is used with the Perfect Tense in Latin, where in English we would use the Pluperfect.

EXERCISE 154.
1. We ascended the steps of the beautiful temple.
2. Caesar attacked on[1] the left wing.
3. Our men did not withstand the enemy's attack.
4. After the war the army reached home.
5. By the consent of the Senate the people chose a king.
6. The women fell on to their knees and begged for peace.
7. The young men dragged the maidens from the hands of their parents.
8. Open (pl.) the door of the house.
9. The boldness of Mucius pleased the Senate.
10. When Suetonius led his troops to Anglesey, not even the women stayed at home.

[1] ā with Abl.

EXERCISE 155.
Among the hostages the Romans had handed over to the king of the Etruscans a brave maiden, Cloelia by name. By chance the guards were not looking at the hostages; Cloelia therefore led a band of her companions to the bank of the Tiber; from there they swam across the river and reached home. Porsenna at once sent messengers to the Senate. However, admiration soon overcame his anger. 'If', said he, 'you hand over to me the hostage Cloelia, I will send her back safe.' When Cloelia again reached the camp of the Etruscans, Porsenna not only praised her, but sent her back with a large part of the hostages.

Derivation Test

1. **Cornū.**   2. **Gradus.**   3. **Impetus.**   4. **Manus.**

Chapter 31

1st and 2nd Conjugations: Different forms of Perfect Base

Many Verbs of the 1st and 2nd Conjugations have been met already which are quite regular in the formation of their Perfect Base, e.g. in the 1st Conjug. **nuntiāvī, fugāvī, monstrāvī**; in the 2nd Conjug. **pārui, timuī, placuī.**

Some quite common Verbs, however, of these two Conjugations have a Perfect Base which is not the Regular Base of their own Conjugation: they use a Base like that of another Conjugation.

Here are some Irregular Verbs of the 1st and 2nd Conjugations: it will easily be seen from what other Conjugation they have borrowed their Perfect Base:

1st Conjugation.

Present Tense	Perfect Tense	
secō	secuī	*I cut*
sonō	sonuī	*I sound*
vetō	vetuī	*I forbid*
iuvō	iūvī	*I help*
dō	dedī	*I give*
stō	stetī	*I stand*

2nd Conjugation.

The original type of 2nd Conjug. Perfect Base and Ending was -ēvī, not -uī.

dēleō	dēlēvī	*I destroy*
impleō	implēvī	*I fill*
ardeō	arsī	*I am on fire*
augeō	auxī	*I increase* (tr.)
fulgeō	fulsī	*I shine*

haereō	haesī	*I stick* (intr.)
iubeō	iussī	*I order*
maneō	mansī	*I remain*
rīdeō	rīsī	*I laugh*
respondeō	respondī	*I answer*
caveō	cāvī	*I am on my guard (against)*
moveō	mōvī	*I move* (tr.)
sedeō	sēdī	*I sit*
obsideō (compound of sedeō)	obsēdī	*I besiege*
videō	vīdī	*I see*

Numerals

Here are two classes of Numeral Adjectives. Cardinal Numbers express simple Number (1, 2, 3, etc.); Ordinal Numbers express the order of Number (1st, 2nd, 3rd, etc.):

	Roman Numerals	Cardinals	Ordinals
1	I	ūnus, -a, -um	prīmus, -a, -um, *first*
2	II	duo, duae, duo	secundus, etc., *second,*
3	III	trēs, tria	tertius, etc.
4	IV	quattuor	quartus
5	V	quinque	quintus
6	VI	sex	sextus
7	VII	septem	septimus
8	VIII	octō	octāvus
9	IX	novem	nōnus
10	X	decem	decimus
11	XI	undecim	undecimus
12	XII	duodecim	duodecimus

None of the above Cardinals is declined except the first three, which are declined below; all the Ordinals are declined like **bonus**.

Base   ūn-, *one*.

Sing.	M.	F.	N.	Plur.	M.	F.	N.
Nom.	ūnus	ūna	ūnum		ūnī	ūnae	ūna
Voc.	ūne	ūna	ūnum		ūnī	ūnae	ūna
Acc.	ūnum	ūnam	ūnum		ūnōs	ūnās	ūna
Gen.	ūnīus	ūnīus	ūnīus		ūnōrum	ūnārum	ūnōrum
Dat.	ūnī	ūnī	ūnī		ūnīs	ūnīs	ūnīs
Abl.	ūnō	ūnā	ūnō		ūnīs	ūnīs	ūnīs

Like **ūnus** are declined: **sōlus**, *only, alone*; **tōtus**, *whole*; **nullus**, *no, none*. **Ūnus** is used in the plur. with plur. Nouns which have a sing. meaning, e.g. **ūna castra**, *one camp*.

	duo, *two*.				trēs, *three*.	
	M.	F.	N.		M. and F.	N.
Nom.	duo	duae	duo		trēs	tria
Voc.	duo	duae	duo		trēs	tria
Acc.	duōs (or duo)	duās	duo		trēs or trīs	tria
Gen.	duōrum	duārum	duōrum		trium	trium
Dat.	duōbus	duābus	duōbus		tribus	tribus
Abl.	duōbus	duābus	duōbus		tribus	tribus

Like **duo** is declined: **ambō**, *both*.

With Numerals and words expressing Number, **ē** or **ex** with the Abl. are often used rather than a Genitive:

Ūnus ex obsidibus, *one of the hostages*.
Nēmō ē captīvīs, *none of the captives*.

EXERCISE 156.

1. Romani urbem in septem montibus aedificaverunt.
2. Secunda legio Glevi manebat.
3. Claudius quattuor legiones ad Britanniam misit.
4. Claudius undecim reges Britanniae[1] vicit.
5. Veni, vidi, vici.[2]
6. Quod Horatius ita iusserat, nullus miles e toto exercitu cum eo manserat.

[1] This information is given on a triumphal arch, found in Rome.
[2] Written in a despatch by Julius Caesar after a victory in Asia in 47 B.C.

7. Caesar Androclo veniam dedit.
8. Horatius cum duobus comitibus in ponte mansit.
9. Barbari nonam legionem noctu oppugnaverant.
10. Britanni multa ex oppidis vastaverunt.

EXERCISE 157.

A BRAVE BROTHER

In the reign of Tullus Hostilius (673-642 B.C.) it was decided that a war between Rome and neighbouring Alba, chief of the cities forming the Latin League, should be settled by a single combat between three Roman brothers, called Horatii, and three Alban brothers, called Curiatii.

Sex fratres ad pugnam se armant et feroces inter duos exercitus procedunt. Ubi praeco signum dedit, proelium commiserunt. Ut arma sonuerunt et gladii fulserunt, pavor ingens ambos exercitus implet. Mox oculis eorum apparent et vulnera et sanguis; fratres Romani tres Albanos vulneraverant, duo tamen ex Romanis ceciderunt et exspiraverunt. Albanus exercitus propter eorum casum laetus exclamabat; exercitus Romanus, ubi Albani unum reliquum circumsteterunt, desperabat. Forte is salvus erat et consilio sapienti se fugae mandabat. Post breve spatium unum Albanorum (neque a tergo procul aberat) vidit. Magno impetu se convertit et eum oppugnavit; dum Albanus exercitus duos reliquos ad auxilium vocat, Horatius hostem occidit et secundam pugnam petivit. Tum Romani clamore adiuvant militem suum. Dum tertius Albanus non procul abest, Romanus secundum occidit. Iam supersunt solum duo iuvenes. Romanus exsultat: 'Duos,' inquit, 'fratrum Manibus[1] dedi: tertium deo belli dabo.' Albanus iam saucius arma vix sustinebat; Romanus eum gladio occidit.

[1] **Mānēs, -ium** (m.), *departed spirits*.

EXERCISE 158.

1. The Romans increased their territory by war.
2. The Iceni nearly destroyed the ninth legion.
3. The Romans elected two consuls.

4. The weapons had all stuck in Horatius's shield.
5. Porsenna in vain besieged the city.
6. Horatius sent back both his companions.
7. Both the legions were in one camp.
8. Seven kings had reigned in the city of Rome.
9. The Sabines did not give Tarpeia gold, as they had promised.
10. When the king sent Cloelia back, the Etruscans struck[1] camp.

[1] *I strike camp*, **castra moveō.**

EXERCISE 159.

The three Roman brothers and the three Alban brothers prepared themselves for the fight and advanced between the armies, as the two kings had ordered. When they heard the signal, they began to fight with each other. Soon two of the Romans were lying dead upon the ground. This victory roused the shouts of the Albans; the Romans, sad because of the death of the two young men, were silent. But the remaining brother pretended flight and suddenly turned round and killed one of the Albans; then he killed the second brother, finally he killed the third. Thus the Romans won a victory by the bravery of one man.

Derivation Test

(*a*) 1. **Duo.**   2. **Decimus.**   3. **Augeō.**   4. **Ambō.**

(*b*) 1. Total.   2. Sanguine.   3. Procedure.   4. December.

Chapter 32

5th Declension

The Stem of Nouns of the 5th Declension ends in -ē. This letter appears in all the Cases.

Stem	diē- *day* (m.).	rē- *thing, event, affair* (f.).
Sing.		
Nom.	diēs	rēs
Voc.	diēs	rēs
Acc.	diem	rem
Gen.	diēī	reī
Dat.	diēī	reī
Abl.	diē	rē
Plur.		
Nom.	diēs	rēs
Voc.	diēs	rēs
Acc.	diēs	rēs
Gen.	diērum	rērum
Dat.	diēbus	rēbus
Abl.	diēbus	rēbus

Diēs is sometimes fem. (in the sing. only), when it means an appointed day: **certā diē vēnērunt,** *they came on the appointed day.*

Diēs and **rēs** are the only two Nouns of this Decl. which are declined throughout.

Like **diēs** (with a long **e** in Gen. and Dat. sing.) are declined: **aciēs** (f.) *line of battle* (in plur., Nom. and Acc. only); **merīdiēs** (m.), *noon* (in sing. only).

Like **rēs** (with a short **e** in Gen. and Dat. sing.) are declined: **spēs** (f.), *hope* (in plur., Nom. and Acc. only); **fidēs** (f.), *faith, loyalty, pledge* (in sing. only).

A compound word **rēspublica,** *state, commonwealth,* is declined in full in both parts, **rempublicam, reīpublicae,** etc.

Ways of Expressing Time
(1) Length of Time (How long?)

Length of Time is expressed by the Accusative:

Agricola prōvinciam Britanniam septem annōs administrāvit.

Agricola governed Britain for seven years.

If the length of time is emphasized, **per** is sometimes used as well:

Per decem annōs Graecī Trōiam obsidēbant.
The Greeks were besieging Troy for ten years.

(2) Point of Time (When?)

A definite Point of Time is expressed by the Ablative:

Sextō annō Agricola Calēdoniam penetrāvit.
In his sixth year (as governor) Agricola penetrated Caledonia.

Posterō diē Britannī nostrōs equitēs oppugnābant.
On the next day the Britons began to attack our cavalry.

Posterō diē was often made into one word, **postrīdiē.**

The Romans divided daylight and darkness into twelve hours (**hōrae**) each, so that the length of hours varied at different times of the year. The sixth hour of the day always ended at noon. The night was divided into four watches (**vigiliae**) of three hours each; the second watch would end at midnight.

Thus **nōnā hōrā diēī** would correspond to what we call 3 p.m. (post merīdiem), and **tertiā ferē vigiliā** would be *at about midnight,* though the times will not be the same as ours because of the difference (*a*) in longitude, (*b*) in the length of hours.

(3) Limit of Time (Within what time?)

The Ablative is also used to express the Limit of Time within which someone does something:

Quattuor diēbus equitēs ad Britanniam pervēnerant.
Within four days the cavalry had reached Britain.

Mōmentō temporis Sabīnī arcem intrāverant.
In a moment the Sabines had entered the citadel.

The following diagram may be of help in remembering the ways of expressing Time in Latin:

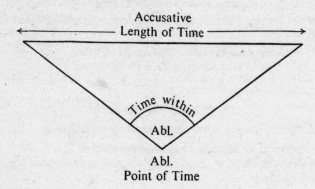

Accusative
Length of Time

Time within

Abl.

Abl.
Point of Time

EXERCISE 160.

1. Caesar quarta hora diei ad Britanniam pervenit.
2. Romulus multos annos regnavit.
3. Agricola in fide Britannorum spem habebat.
4. Horatii et Curiatii inter duas acies processerunt.
5. Romani rempublicam dictatori[1] interdum mandabant.
6. Et Romani et Porsenna fidem conservaverunt.
7. Ante meridiem totum librum legeram.
8. Tarpeia Romam prodidit: ea res erat turpis.

[1] A dictator was the chief magistrate, armed with absolute power, elected by the Romans in times of emergency for a period of six months. An example of such a dictator is Camillus, in the next Exercise.

  9. Sex dies labora, septimo requiesce.
10. Romani paucis annis magnam Britanniae partem super-
     averant.

EXERCISE 161.

MINING OPERATIONS IN A SIEGE

*There were constant wars between Rome and the Etruscan
city of Vēii, which was only 12 miles away. The final war broke
out in 406 B.C. After slow progress for several years, the Romans
elected Camillus dictator, to meet the emergency. Veii had been
besieged all the time and fell in 396 B.C.*

Milites in arcem hostium multos dies cuniculum agunt,
neque opus intermittunt. Sub terra continuus labor eos non
fatigat; Camillus enim milites in sex partes dividit; sexta modo
pars uno tempore laborat et sex modo horas in opere manet.
Tandem dictator die certa ab omnibus locis magna cum mul-
titudine urbem oppugnat. Ita cives magnum cuniculi periculum non sentiunt. Ut fabula narrat, Romani milites vocem
sacerdotis Veientis (ante proelium enim sacrificabat) in cuniculo exaudiunt.

Subito e cuniculo, delectis militibus[1] pleno, in arcem
evolaverunt armati; pars muros petiverunt,[2] pars claustra
portarum revellerunt, pars adhibuerunt ignes. Ita rem decer-
nunt. Clamor militum et ploratus mulierum ac[3] puerorum
omnia implent; nulla spes civibus superest. Momento temporis
Romani ex muro armatos deturbant, portas aperiunt; inde
agmen intrat et totam urbem in potestatem suam redigit. Tum
iussu dictatoris Romani ab inermibus abstinent. Is finis
sanguinis fuit.

    [1] plēnus, *full*, is used with either Gen. or Abl.
    [2] With Nouns denoting a number of people (Collective Nouns),
a plur. Verb is often used.
    [3] ac (before Consonants only) and atque are often used to express
and.

EXERCISE 162.

  1. On the fourth night the moon was full.
  2. Calgacus had drawn up his line of battle.

3. Agricola's troops fought for many hours.
4. On the next day the enemy gave Agricola hostages.
5. The Romans placed their hope on one man, Horatius.
6. The Roman state was in danger for many years.
7. In a moment the Sabines had entered the Roman citadel.
8. The scout reported many things to Caesar within five days.
9. The Romans gave a pledge to the Etruscans.
10. Caesar departed at about the third watch.

EXERCISE 163.

For many days and nights the Roman soldiers had been working in the tunnel, but they did not all work at one time; therefore they were not tired. There was a temple of Juno in the citadel; in this temple (if the story is worthy of belief) a priest was sacrificing before the fight. At that time the Romans had reached the wall of the temple and overheard the priest's voice.

When Camillus gave the signal, some of the Romans flew out from the tunnel to the walls, some to the gates; some began to burn the houses. Within a short time the city of Veii was in the hands of the Romans; they had besieged it for ten years.

Derivation Test

1. Momentary. 2. Partial. 3. Cloister. 4. Republican.

Chapter 33

Adjectives of 3rd Declension with Consonant Stems

There are only a few 3rd Decl. Adjectives with Stems ending in a Consonant: they have the same ending for the Nom. sing. in all genders, but they are rarely used in the neuter at all.

Stem   veter-, *old*.

Sing.	M. and F.	N.	*Plur.* M. and F.	N.
Nom.	vetus	vetus	veterēs	vetera
Voc.	vetus	vetus	veterēs	vetera
Acc.	veterem	vetus	veterēs	vetera
Gen.	veteris		veterum	
Dat.	veterī		veteribus	
Abl.	vetere		veteribus	

Vetus is the only Adjective of this type which has Nom., Voc., and Acc. neuter plural.

Other Adjectives of this type are: **dīves (dīvit-)**, *rich*; **pauper (pauper-)**, *poor*; **inops (inop-)**, *helpless*; **memor (memor-)**, *mindful*; **immemor (immemor-)**, *forgetful*. **Inops, memor, immemor** have Abl. sing. in-**ī**.

Present Infinitive Active of the Four Conjugations

The **Infinitive** of a Verb expresses a general activity or state, without any alteration in its ending to denote Person or Number. **Pugnant**, *they fight*, has an ending which shows both Person and Number; **pugnāre**, *to fight*, has an ending which is not bounded (**infīnītus**) by Person or Number. An example will make this clear:

Pugnāre constituit, *he determined to fight*.
Pugnāre constituimus, *we determined to fight*.

Pugnāre remains unchanged, though the Persons and Numbers of those who *determined* to fight are different.

The Present Infinitives of the Four Conjugations are formed by adding **-re** to the Verb-Stem (**-ere** to Consonant Stems of the 3rd Conjugation).

Conjugation	Pres. Ind.	Verb-Stem	Pres. Infin.
1st	**amō**	**amā-**	**amā-re**
2nd	**moneō**	**monē-**	**monē-re**
3rd	**regō**	**reg-**	**reg-e-re**
4th	**audiō**	**audī-**	**audī-re**

Prolative Infinitive

Many Verbs require another Verb in the Infinitive to complete their sense: this Infinitive is sometimes called a Prolative Infinitive, because it *carries forward* the sense of the Verb before it.

The following Verbs are often found with a Prolative Infinitive (the figure in brackets is the number of their Conjugation):

properō (1), *I hasten.*
dubitō (1), *I hesitate.*
audeō (2), *I dare.*
dēbeō (2), *I ought.*
soleō (2), *I am accustomed.*

timeō (2), *I am afraid.*
constituō (3), *I resolve.*
dēsistō (3), *I cease.*
discō (3), *I learn.*
sciō (4), *I know (how to).*

Gallī domum pervenīre properābant (constituerant).
The Gauls were hastening (had resolved) to reach home.

Explōrātor sē barbarīs mandāre timēbat.
The scout was afraid to entrust himself to the rough natives.

Scīsne natāre? *Do you know how to swim?*

EXERCISE 164.

1. Suetonius copias Londinium ducere properavit.
2. Memor multorum periculorum, dux Londinium relinquere constituit.
3. Homines divites pauperes iuvare debent.
4. Britanni auxilium Gallis dare solebant.

5. Propter hiemem et tempestates Caesar in Britannia manere timebat.
6. Dominum inopem Bucephalas e periculo reportavit.
7. Romani coloniam militum veterum Camuloduni collocaverunt.
8. Aestate pueri natare discunt.
9. Per anuli beneficium Gyges dives esse constituit.
10. Quod Mettius erat in tanto periculo, Sabini pugnare destiterant.

EXERCISE 165.

CAMILLUS AND THE SCHOOLMASTER (1)

Besides Veii, other Etruscan States made war on Rome, including the Falisci, who surrendered their city, Falerii, in 394. An interesting account is given by Livy of what led to the surrender.

Principes Faliscorum curae unius magistri liberos solebant mandare. Is in pace pueros ludorum causa extra urbem ducere instituerat neque eum morem per belli tempus intermisit. Ludos et sermonem cotidie variat; intervallo[1] modo longo, modo brevi eos ab urbis porta trahit. Tandem inter stationes hostium et castra Romana in praetorium Camilli eos ducere audet. 'Falerios', inquit, 'in manus Romanorum tradidi; parentes enim eorum puerorum sunt ibi principes.' Camillus, ubi ea audivit, 'Neque ad populum neque ad imperatorem similem tui scelestus cum scelesto munere venisti. Nos cum Faliscis societatem non confirmavimus; per naturam tamen societas est eritque. Sunt iura non modo pacis sed etiam belli; ea conservare didicimus. Arma habemus non adversus pueros inopes, sed adversus armatos. Tu novo scelere vicisti; ego virtute et armis vincam.'

[1] *at a distance*: **intervallō** is an Abl. of Manner, showing *how* something is done, rather like Abl. of Instrument.

EXERCISE 166.

1. After the death of Romulus, the people did not cease to demand a king.

2. The Romans were good soldiers, because they had learnt to obey.
3. The poor began to demand freedom in Rome after the war.
4. Horatius did not hesitate to defend the bridge.
5. Clever men do not always know how to teach.
6. All the citizens, rich and poor, hastened to give Horatius a reward.
7. Agricola determined to conquer the inhabitants of Caledonia.
8. The Britons were accustomed to fight from chariots.
9. At first Androclus does not dare to look at the huge lion.
10. Caesar was afraid to disembark his troops at Dover.

EXERCISE 167.

At Falerii one schoolmaster was accustomed to teach all the children of the chief citizens. Once the Falisci were waging war, but even then he exercised the boys outside the walls of the city; sometimes for this purpose,[1] as he pretended, he led them far from the gate. He had really[2] determined to lead them into the enemy's camp. At last he penetrated the outposts of the Romans and led the children into the dictator's tent. 'Through me', said he, 'Falerii is now in your hands; these are the children of the chiefs of the Falisci.' Camillus, angry because of this wicked deed, replied: 'We are not accustomed to wage war against helpless children; we have not established an alliance with the Falisci, but nature has established her own alliance between all men.'

[1] *for the sake of this thing.*
[2] *really*, rē vērā (sometimes as one word, rēvērā).

Derivation Test

1. **Vetus.**   2. **Tempestās.**   3. **Princeps.**   4. **Rēs.**

Chapter 34

3rd Declension : Irregular Nouns

There are a few Nouns of the 3rd Declension which do not altogether follow the regular types.

	senex *old man* (m.).	bōs *ox, cow* (c.).	sūs *pig* (c.).	Iuppiter *Jupiter* (m.).	vīs *force, violence* (f.).
Sing.					
Nom.	senex	bōs	sūs	Iuppiter	vīs
Voc.	senex	bōs	sūs	Iuppiter	(no Voc.)
Acc.	senem	bovem	suem	Iovem	vim
Gen.	senis	bovis	suis	Iovis	—
Dat.	senī	bovī	suī	Iovī	—
Abl.	sene	bove	sue	Iove	vī
Plur.					
N.V.	senēs	bovēs	suēs	no plur.	vīrēs
Acc.	senēs	bovēs	suēs		vīrēs
Gen.	senum	boum	suum		vīrium
Dat.	senibus	bōbus or	suibus or		vīribus
Abl.	senibus	būbus	subus		vīribus

Like sūs is declined grūs (c.), *crane*, except that Dat. and Abl. plur. are always gruibus. Vīrēs means *strength*.

	iter *journey, march, route* (n.)		
Sing.		*Plur.*	
N.V.A.	iter	itinera	
Gen.	itineris	itinerum	
Dat.	itinerī	itineribus	
Abl.	itinere	itineribus	

Negative Commands

Negative Commands (often called Prohibitions) are expressed by using the 2nd pers. sing., **nōlī,** or the 2nd pers. plur., **nōlīte,** of the Imperative of the Verb **nōlō,** *I am unwilling,* followed by the Present Infinitive:

Nōlī amicōs neglegere.
Do not neglect your friends.

Nōlīte Rōmānōrum iniūriās tolerāre.
Do not put up with the wrongdoings of the Romans.

Infinitive as a Noun

(*a*) The Infinitive is often used as a Noun:

Vidēre est crēdere.
Seeing is believing.

(*b*) When the Infinitive is used as a Noun, its gender is neuter:

Natāre nōn est difficile.
Swimming is not difficult, or, *it is not difficult to swim.*

(*c*) Even when the Infinitive is used as a Noun, it can still govern an Object:

Falsa dīcere est turpe.
Telling lies is disgraceful, or, *it is disgraceful to tell lies.*

EXERCISE 168.
1. Hercules vocem boum audivit.
2. Erant Herculi vires magnae.
3. Magnis itineribus Agricola in Caledoniam contendit.
4. Laborare est orare.
5. Senatus erat concilium senum.
6. Nolite inermes oppugnare.
7. Saepe Romani suem et ovem et taurum Iovi immolabant.
8. Noli praemium exspectare, nisi laboraveris.
9. Ludos spectare Romanos delectabat.
10. Non erat facile Caesari copias in Britanniam exponere.

EXERCISE 169.

CAMILLUS AND THE SCHOOLMASTER (2)

Deinde milites iussu Camilli manus magistri post tergum vinciunt. Camillus pueris eum tradidit virgasque eis dedit. 'Proditorem,' inquit, 'Falerios reducite, verberate, agite in urbem.' Ibi primum multi cives ad id spectaculum concurrunt; deinde magistratus de re tam nova senatum vocant. Omnes cives fidem Romanam, iustitiam dictatoris, et in foro et in curia celebrant pacemque postulant; inde legatos Romam ad senatum mittunt. Ei, ubi ad senatum venerunt, 'Et vos', inquiunt, 'et imperator vester nos vicistis; neque dei neque homines ei victoriae invidebunt. Vos fidem in bello conservavistis, nos ea fides ad deditionem provocavit. Itaque sub imperio vestro, non sub legibus nostris, nunc nobis placet vivere. Et obsides et arma vobis dedere parati sumus; portae urbis exercitui vestro patebunt.'

EXERCISE 170.

1. The force of the storm drove back Caesar's ships.
2. Food supplies strength to the body.
3. It is pleasant to read books.
4. Young men have strength, old men have wisdom.
5. The Etruscans attempted a way across the bridge by force.
6. Do (pl.) not advance, unless you see the signal.
7. Obeying is not always easy.
8. Romulus dedicated a temple to Jupiter.
9. By forced marches Suetonius soon reached London.
10. Don't (s.) walk on the grass.

EXERCISE 171.

The boys drove their schoolmaster home, as the dictator had commanded. When they entered the city, they hurried to seek the magistrates and to hand over the traitor. Meanwhile many citizens were running through the streets to the strange sight. Then the magistrates called the senate; the senators decided to send ambassadors to Rome and to ask for peace.

'It is just', they say, 'to surrender our city to the Romans: such men know how to keep faith even in war. They have conquered us, not by force, but by justice, and we and the Roman people will hand down a good example to the human race.'

Derivation Test

1. Bovine.   2. Jovial.   3. Itinerant.   4. Tradition.

Summary of Grammar

Nouns

1st Declension

Sing.   *Plur.*

	Sing.	Plur.
Nom.	mensa (f.), *table*	mensae
Voc.	mensa	mensae
Acc.	mensam	mensās
Gen.	mensae	mensārum
Dat.	mensae	mensīs
Abl.	mensā	mensīs

Note. Fīlia, *daughter*, and dea, *goddess*, have Dat. and Abl. plur. fīliābus, deābus.

2nd Declension

Sing.

Nom.	dominus (m.), *master*	magister (m.), *master*	puer (m.),
Voc.	domine (*of household*)	magister (*of school*)	puer [*boy*
Acc.	dominum	magistrum	puerum
Gen.	dominī	magistrī	puerī
Dat.	dominō	magistrō	puerō
Abl.	dominō	magistrō	puerō

Plur.

Nom.	dominī	magistrī	puerī
Voc.	dominī	magistrī	puerī
Acc.	dominōs	magistrōs	puerōs
Gen.	dominōrum	magistrōrum	puerōrum
Dat.	dominīs	magistrīs	puerīs
Abl.	dominīs	magistrīs	puerīs

Note. Fīlius, *son*, has Voc. sing. fīlī, and Gen. sing. fīlī or fīliī; deus, *god*, has Voc. sing. deus; vir, *man*, keeps vir- throughout.

	Sing.	Plur.
Nom.	bellum (n.), *war*	bella
Voc.	bellum	bella
Acc.	bellum	bella
Gen.	bellī	bellōrum
Dat.	bellō	bellīs
Abl.	bellō	bellīs

Note. Neuter Nouns in **-ium**, e.g. **auxilium**, *help*, form Gen. sing. in **-ī** or **-iī**.

3rd Declension

(1) Nouns with Consonant Stems

Sing.

	rex (m.), *king*	mīles (c.), *soldier*	consul (m.), *consul*
Nom.	rex	mīles	consul
Voc.	rex	mīles	consul
Acc.	rēgem	mīlitem	consulem
Gen.	rēgis	mīlitis	consulis
Dat.	rēgī	mīlitī	consulī
Abl.	rēge	mīlite	consule

Plur.

Nom.	rēgēs	mīlitēs	consulēs
Voc.	rēgēs	mīlitēs	consulēs
Acc.	rēgēs	mīlitēs	consulēs
Gen.	rēgum	mīlitum	consulum
Dat.	rēgibus	mīlitibus	consulibus
Abl.	rēgibus	mīlitibus	consulibus

	Sing.	Plur.
Nom.	leō (m.), *lion*	leōnēs
Voc.	leō	leōnēs
Acc.	leōnem	leōnēs
Gen.	leōnis	leōnum
Dat.	leōnī	leōnibus
Abl.	leōne	leōnibus

Sing.

Nom.	caput (n.), *head*	opus (n.), *work*	carmen (n.) *song*
Voc.	caput	opus	carmen
Acc.	caput	opus	carmen
Gen.	capitis	operis	carminis
Dat.	capitī	operī	carminī
Abl.	capite	opere	carmine

Plur.

Nom.	capita	opera	carmina
Voc.	capita	opera	carmina
Acc.	capita	opera	carmina
Gen.	capitum	operum	carminum
Dat.	capitibus	operibus	carminibus
Abl.	capitibus	operibus	carminibus

(2) Nouns with I- Stems

(a) Nom. sing. in -is, -er, or -ēs

Sing.

Nom.	hostis (c.), *enemy*	imber (m.), *shower*	nūbēs (f.), *cloud*
Voc.	hostis	imber	nūbēs
Acc.	hostem	imbrem	nūbem
Gen.	hostis	imbris	nūbis
Dat.	hostī	imbrī	nūbī
Abl.	hoste	imbre	nūbe

Plur.

Nom.	hostēs	imbrēs	nūbēs
Voc.	hostēs	imbrēs	nūbēs
Acc.	hostēs (or -īs)	imbrēs (or -īs)	nūbēs (or -īs)
Gen.	hostium	imbrium	nūbium
Dat.	hostibus	imbribus	nūbibus
Abl.	hostibus	imbribus	nūbibus

Note. Pater, patris, *father*; māter, mātris, *mother*; frāter, frātris, *brother*, have Gen. pl. in -um; so also iuvenis (c.), *young person*, and canis (c.), *dog*. Abl. of ignis (m.), *fire*, is usually ignī.

(b) Neuter

Sing.

Nom.	cubīle (n.), *couch*	animal (n.), *animal*	calcar (n.), *spur*
Voc.	cubīle	animal	calcar
Acc.	cubīle	animal	calcar
Gen.	cubīlis	animālis	calcāris
Dat.	cubīlī	animālī	calcārī
Abl.	cubīlī	animālī	calcārī

Plur.

Nom.	cubīlia	animālia	calcāria
Voc.	cubīlia	animālia	calcāria
Acc.	cubīlia	animālia	calcāria
Gen.	cubīlium	animālium	calcārium
Dat.	cubīlibus	animālibus	calcāribus
Abl.	cubīlibus	animālibus	calcāribus

(c) Nom. sing. of one syllable, ending in two consonants; also Nom. ending in -tās

Sing.

Nom.	urbs (f.), *city*	pons (m.), *bridge*	cīvitās (f.), *state*
Voc.	urbs	pons	cīvitās
Acc.	urbem	pontem	cīvitātem
Gen.	urbis	pontis	cīvitātis
Dat.	urbī	pontī	cīvitātī
Abl.	urbe	ponte	cīvitāte

Plur.

Nom.	urbēs	pontēs	cīvitātēs
Voc.	urbēs	pontēs	cīvitātēs
Acc.	urbēs (or -īs)	pontēs (or -īs)	cīvitātēs (or -īs)
Gen.	urbium	pontium	cīvitātium
Dat.	urbibus	pontibus	cīvitātibus
Abl.	urbibus	pontibus	cīvitātibus

Note. Nox, noctis (f.), *night*, is declined in the same way.

(3) Irregular Nouns

Sing.

Nom.	senex (m.), *old*	bōs (c.), *ox*	sūs (c.), *pig*	Iuppiter (m.),
Voc.	senex [*man*	bōs	sūs	Iuppiter [*Jupiter*
Acc.	senem	bovem	suem	Iovem
Gen.	senis	bovis	suis	Iovis
Dat.	senī	bovī	suī	Iovī
Abl.	sene	bove	sue	Iove

Plur.

Nom.	senēs	bovēs	suēs	
Voc.	senēs	bovēs	suēs	no plur.
Acc.	senēs	bovēs	suēs	
Gen.	senum	boum	suum	
Dat.	senibus	⎰bōbus or	⎰suibus or	
Abl.	senibus	⎱būbus	⎱subus	

	Sing.	*Plur.*
Nom.	vīs (f.), *force*	vīrēs (*strength*)
Voc.	—	vīrēs
Acc.	vim	vīrēs
Gen.	—	vīrium
Dat.	—	vīribus
Abl.	vī	vīribus

	Sing.	*Plur.*
N.V.A.	iter (n.), *journey*	itinera
Gen.	itineris	itinerum
Dat.	itinerī	itineribus
Abl.	itinere	itineribus

4th Declension

	Sing.	*Plur.*
Nom.	gradus (m.), *step*	gradūs
Voc.	gradus	gradūs
Acc.	gradum	gradūs
Gen.	gradūs	graduum
Dat.	graduī	gradibus
Abl.	gradū	gradibus

Sing.			Plur.
N.V.A.	cornū (n.), *horn*		cornua
Gen.	cornūs		cornuum
Dat.	cornū		cornibus
Abl.	cornū		cornibus

Note. **Domus** (f.), *house,* can be declined like **gradus** in all Cases except in the Abl. where it takes the form **domō.**

5th Declension

Sing.		Plur.	Sing.		Plur.
Nom.	diēs (m.), *day*	diēs	rēs (f.), *thing*		rēs
Voc.	diēs	diēs	rēs		rēs
Acc.	diem	diēs	rem		rēs
Gen.	diēī	diērum	reī		rērum
Dat.	diēī	diēbus	reī		rēbus
Abl.	diē	diēbus	rē		rēbus

Adjectives

(1) 1st and 2nd Declensions

(a) in -us, -a, -um: bonus, *good*

Sing.	M.	F.	N.
Nom.	bonus	bona	bonum
Voc.	bone	bona	bonum
Acc.	bonum	bonam	bonum
Gen.	bonī	bonae	bonī
Dat.	bonō	bonae	bonō
Abl.	bonō	bonā	bonō

Plur.			
Nom.	bonī	bonae	bona
Voc.	bonī	bonae	bona
Acc.	bonōs	bonās	bona
Gen.	bonōrum	bonārum	bonōrum
Dat.	bonīs	bonīs	bonīs
Abl.	bonīs	bonīs	bonīs

Note. **meus,** *my,* has Voc. sing. masc. **mī.**

Adjectives

173

(b) in -er, -ra, -rum: niger, *black*

Sing.	M.	F.	N.
Nom.	niger	nigra	nigrum
Voc.	niger	nigra	nigrum
Acc.	nigrum	nigram	nigrum
Gen.	nigrī	nigrae	nigrī
Dat.	nigrō	nigrae	nigrō
Abl.	nigrō	nigrā	nigrō

Plur.			
Nom.	nigrī	nigrae	nigra
Voc.	nigrī	nigrae	nigra
Acc.	nigrōs	nigrās	nigra
Gen.	nigrōrum	nigrārum	nigrōrum
Dat.	nigrīs	nigrīs	nigrīs
Abl.	nigrīs	nigrīs	nigrīs

(c) in -er, -era, -erum: tener, *tender*

Sing.	M.	F.	N.
Nom.	tener	tenera	tenerum
Voc.	tener	tenera	tenerum
Acc.	tenerum	teneram	tenerum
Gen.	tenerī	tenerae	tenerī
Dat.	tenerō	tenerae	tenerō
Abl.	tenerō	tenerā	tenerō

Plur.			
Nom.	tenerī	tenerae	tenera
Voc.	tenerī	tenerae	tenera
Acc.	tenerōs	tenerās	tenera
Gen.	tenerōrum	tenerārum	tenerōrum
Dat.	tenerīs	tenerīs	tenerīs
Abl.	tenerīs	tenerīs	tenerīs

(2) 3rd Declension

(i) I-Stems

    (a) with three endings in Nom. sing. : ācer, *keen*

Sing.	M.	F.	N.
Nom.	ācer	ācris	ācre
Voc.	ācer	ācris	ācre
Acc.	ācrem	ācrem	ācre
Gen.	ācris	ācris	ācris
Dat.	ācrī	ācrī	ācrī
Abl.	ācrī	ācrī	ācrī

Plur.			
Nom.	ācrēs	ācrēs	ācria
Voc.	ācrēs	ācrēs	ācria
Acc.	ācrēs (or -īs)	ācrēs (or -īs)	ācria
Gen.	ācrium	ācrium	ācrium
Dat.	ācribus	ācribus	ācribus
Abl.	ācribus	ācribus	ācribus

Note. Celer, celeris, celere, *swift*, keeps -er throughout, and has Gen. plur. celerum.

    (b) with two endings in Nom. sing. : omnis, *all*

Sing.	M. and F.	N.	Plur. M. and F.	N.
Nom.	omnis	omne	omnēs	omnia
Voc.	omnis	omne	omnēs	omnia
Acc.	omnem	omne	omnēs (or -īs)	omnia
Gen.	omnis	omnis	omnium	omnium
Dat.	omnī	omnī	omnibus	omnibus
Abl.	omnī	omnī	omnibus	omnibus

    (c) with one ending in Nom. sing. : ingens, *huge*

Sing.	M. and F.	N.	Plur. M. and F.	N.
Nom.	ingens	ingens	ingentēs	ingentia
Voc.	ingens	ingens	ingentēs	ingentia
Acc.	ingentem	ingens	ingentēs (or -īs)	ingentia
Gen.	ingentis	ingentis	ingentium	ingentium
Dat.	ingentī	ingentī	ingentibus	ingentibus
Abl.	ingentī	ingentī	ingentibus	ingentibus

fēlix, *fortunate*

Sing.	M. and F.	N.	*Plur.* M. and F.	N.
Nom.	fēlix	fēlix	fēlicēs	fēlicia
Voc.	fēlix	fēlix	fēlicēs	fēlicia
Acc.	fēlicem	fēlix	fēlicēs (or -īs)	fēlicia
Gen.	fēlicis	fēlicis	fēlicium	fēlicium
Dat.	fēlicī	fēlicī	fēlicibus	fēlicibus
Abl.	fēlicī	fēlicī	fēlicibus	fēlicibus

(ii) Consonant Stems

With one ending in Nom. sing.: **vetus,** *old*

Sing.	M. and F.	N.	*Plur.* M. and F.	N.
Nom.	vetus	vetus	veterēs	vetera
Voc.	vetus	vetus	veterēs	vetera
Acc.	veterem	vetus	veterēs	vetera
Gen.	veteris		veterum	
Dat.	veterī		veteribus	
Abl.	vetere		veteribus	

Note. **Inops, inopis,** *poor;* **memor, memoris,** *mindful;* **immemor, immemoris,** *forgetful,* have Abl. sing. in **-ī.**

Numerals

	Roman Numerals	Cardinals	Ordinals
1	I	ūnus, -a, -um	prīmus, -a, -um, *first*
2	II	duo, duae, duo	secundus, etc., *second,*
3	III	trēs, tria	tertius etc.
4	IV	quattuor	quartus
5	V	quinque	quintus
6	VI	sex	sextus
7	VII	septem	septimus
8	VIII	octō	octāvus
9	IX	novem	nōnus
10	X	decem	decimus
11	XI	undecim	undecimus
12	XII	duodecim	duodecimus

Sing.	M.	F.	N.
Nom.	ūnus	ūna	ūnum
Voc.	ūne	ūna	ūnum
Acc.	ūnum	ūnam	ūnum
Gen.	ūnīus	ūnīus	ūnīus
Dat.	ūnī	ūnī	ūnī
Abl	ūnō	ūnā	ūnō

Note. Plural like **bonus**.

Nom.	duo	duae	duo
Voc.	duo	duae	duo
Acc.	duōs or duo	duās	duo
Gen.	duōrum	duārum	duōrum
Dat.	duōbus	duābus	duōbus
Abl.	duōbus	duābus	duōbus

	M. and F.	N.
Nom.	trēs	tria
Voc.	trēs	tria
Acc.	trēs or trīs	tria
Gen.	trium	trium
Dat.	tribus	tribus
Abl.	tribus	tribus

Pronouns

(1) 1st and 2nd Persons

   (*a*) Personal Pronouns

Sing.		*Plur.*
Nom.	ego, *I*	nōs
Acc.	mē	nōs
Gen.	meī	nostrī, nostrum
Dat.	mihi	nōbīs
Abl.	mē	nōbīs
Nom.	tū, *you* (also Voc.)	vōs (also Voc.)
Acc.	tē	vōs
Gen.	tuī	vestrī, vestrum
Dat.	tibi	vōbīs
Abl.	tē	vōbīs

(*b*) Reflexive Pronouns
As above, omitting the Nom. and Voc.

(*c*) Possessive Pronouns
    1st Person, **meus** (Voc. **mī**), **mea, meum,** *my;*
          noster, nostra, nostrum, *our.*

    2nd Person, **tuus, tua, tuum,** *your* (*of you,* sing.);
          vester, vestra, vestrum, *your* (*of you,* plur.).

(2) 3rd Person
  (*a*) Pronoun
There is no Personal Pronoun for the 3rd Person. Instead, Latin uses the Demonstrative Pronoun, **is, ea, id.**

When used as a Personal Pronoun, **is, ea, id,** means *he, she, it.*

When used as a Demonstrative Pronoun or Adjective, **is, ea, id,** means *this or that* (without emphasis).

Sing.	M.	F.	N.	*Plur.* M.	F.	N.
Nom.	is	ea	id	eī	eae	ea
Acc.	eum	eam	id	eōs	eās	ea
Gen.	ēius	ēius	ēius	eōrum	eārum	eōrum
Dat.	eī	eī	eī	eīs	eīs	eīs
Abl.	eō	eā	eō	eīs	eīs	eīs

  (*b*) Reflexive Pronoun
Sing. and Plur., all genders
Acc.   sē or sēsē, *himself, herself, itself, themselves*
Gen.   suī
Dat.   sibi.
Abl.   sē or sēsē

  (*c*) Possessive Pronouns
(i) ēius (Gen. sing. of **is, ea, id**), *his, her, its*;
   eōrum, eārum, eōrum (Gen. plur. of **is, ea, id**), *their*, when these persons are not the same as the Subject of the sentence in which they occur.
(ii) **suus, sua, suum,** *his own, her own, its own, their own,* when these persons are the same as the Subject of the sentence in which they occur.

Verbs

1. The Verb **sum**

Present Indicative	Present Infinitive	Perfect Indicative
sum, *I am*	**esse,** *to be*	**fuī,** *I was* or *have been*

Indicative Mood

Present Tense	Future Tense	Imperfect Tense
sum	**erō**	**eram**
es	**eris**	**erās**
est	**erit**	**erat**
sumus	**erimus**	**erāmus**
estis	**eritis**	**erātis**
sunt	**erunt**	**erant**

Perfect Tense	Future Perfect Tense	Pluperfect Tense
fuī	**fuerō**	**fueram**
fuistī	**fueris**	**fuerās**
fuit	**fuerit**	**fuerat**
fuimus	**fuerimus**	**fuerāmus**
fuistis	**fueritis**	**fuerātis**
fuērunt	**fuerint**	**fuerant**

2. The Four Conjugations

Indicative Mood Active

	1st Conjug.	2nd Conjug.	3rd Conjug.	4th Conjug.
Present Tense	**amō**	**moneō**	**regō**	**audiō**
Present Infinitive	**amāre**	**monēre**	**regere**	**audīre**
Perfect Tense	**amāvī**	**monuī**	**rexī**	**audīvī**

Tense
Present

amō	**moneō**	**regō**	**audiō**
amās	**monēs**	**regis**	**audīs**
amat	**monet**	**regit**	**audit**
amāmus	**monēmus**	**regimus**	**audīmus**
amātis	**monētis**	**regitis**	**audītis**
amant	**monent**	**regunt**	**audiunt**

Future

amābō	monēbō	regam	audiam
amābis	monēbis	regēs	audiēs
amābit	monēbit	reget	audiet
amābimus	monēbimus	regēmus	audiēmus
amābitis	monēbitis	regētis	audiētis
amābunt	monēbunt	regent	audient

Imperfect

amābam	monēbam	regēbam	audiēbam
amābās	monēbās	regēbās	audiēbās
amābat	monēbat	regēbat	audiēbat
amābāmus	monēbāmus	regēbāmus	audiēbāmus
amābātis	monēbātis	regēbātis	audiēbātis
amābant	monēbant	regēbant	audiēbant

Perfect

amāvī	monuī	rexi	audīvī
amāvistī	monuistī	rexistī	audīvistī
amāvit	monuit	rexit	audīvit
amāvimus	monuimus	reximus	audīvimus
amāvistis	monuistis	rexistis	audīvistis
amāvērunt	monuērunt	rexērunt	audīverunt

Future Perfect

amāverō	monuerō	rexerō	audīverō
amāveris	monueris	rexeris	audīveris
amāverit	monuerit	rexerit	audīverit
amāverimus	monuerimus	rexerimus	audīverimus
amāveritis	monueritis	rexeritis	audīveritis
amāverint	monuerint	rexerint	audīverint

Pluperfect

amāveram	monueram	rexeram	audīveram
amāverās	monuerās	rexerās	audīverās
amāverat	monuerat	rexerat	audīverat
amāverāmus	monuerāmus	rexerāmus	audīverāmus
amāverātis	monuerātis	rexerātis	audīverātis
amāverant	monuerant	rexerant	audīverant

Imperative Active

2nd pers. sing.

  amā   monē   rege   audī

2nd pers. plur.

  amāte   monēte   regite   audīte

Note. **Dūcō** and **dīcō** have **dūc, dīc** for 2nd pers. sing.

3.   Parts of Verbs (some irregular)

(Compounds have the same form, unless stated otherwise)

1st Conjugation

Present	Infinitive	Perfect	
secō	secāre	secuī	*I cut*
sonō	sonāre	sonuī	*I sound*
vetō	vetāre	vetuī	*I forbid*
iuvō	iuvāre	iūvī	*I help*
dō	dare	dedī	*I give*
stō	stāre	stetī	*I stand*

2nd Conjugation

dēleō	dēlēre	dēlēvī	*I destroy*
impleō	implēre	implēvī	*I fill*
ardeō	ardēre	arsī	*I am on fire*
augeō	augēre	auxī	*I increase* (tr.)
fulgeō	fulgēre	fulsī	*I shine*
haereō	haerēre	haesī	*I stick* (intr.)
iubeō	iubēre	iussī	*I order*
maneō	manēre	mansī	*I remain*
rīdeō	rīdēre	rīsī	*I laugh*
respondeō	respondēre	respondī	*I answer*
caveō	cavēre	cāvī	*I am on my guard (against)*
moveō	movēre	mōvī	*I move* (tr.)
sedeō	sedēre	sēdī	*I sit*
obsideō	obsidēre	obsēdī	*I besiege*
videō	vidēre	vīdī	*I see*

3rd Conjugation

intellegō	intellegere	intellexī	*I understand*
neglegō	neglegere	neglexī	*I neglect*
tegō	tegere	texī	*I cover*
dīcō	dīcere	dixī	*I say*
dūcō	dūcere	duxī	*I lead*
gerō	gerere	gessī	*I carry*
instruō	instruere	instruxī	*I draw up*
scrībō	scrībere	scripsī	*I write*
trahō	trahere	traxī	*I drag*
vīvō	vīvere	vixī	*I live*
cēdō	cēdere	cessī	*I go away, yield*
dīvidō	dīvidere	dīvīsī	*I divide*
lūdō	lūdere	lūsī	*I play*
mittō	mittere	mīsī	*I send*
premō	premere	pressī	*I press*
opprimō	opprimere	oppressī	*I overwhelm*
vādō	vādere	(in-)vāsī	*I go, stride, (attack)*
requiescō	requiescere	requiēvī	*I rest*
occumbō	occumbere	occubuī	*I die*
pōnō	pōnere	posuī	*I place*
petō	petere	petīvī	*I seek*
ascendō	ascendere	ascendī	*I climb*
constituō	constituere	constituī	*I determine*

so also: **instituō**, *I begin*; **restituō**, *I restore.*

contendō	contendere	contendī	*I march*
occīdō	occīdere	occīdī	*I kill*
revellō	revellere	revellī	*I pull away*
vertō	vertere	vertī	*I turn* (tr.)

agō	agere	ēgī	*I do, drive*
redigō	redigere	redēgī	*I reduce*
fundō	fundere	fūdī	*I pour*
legō	legere	lēgī	*I read*
ēligō	ēligere	ēlēgī	*I choose*
relinquō	relinquere	relīquī	*I leave*
rumpō	rumpere	rūpī	*I break*
vincō	vincere	vīcī	*I conquer*
addō	addere	addidī	*I add*
cadō	cadere	cecidī	*I fall*
crēdō	crēdere	crēdidī	*I believe*
currō	currere	cucurrī	*I run*

concurrō, perf. concurrī; dēcurrō, perf. usually dēcucurrī

dēdō	dēdere	dēdidī	*I give up*
dēsistō	dēsistere	dēstitī	*I cease*
discō	discere	didicī	*I learn*
pellō	pellere	pepulī	*I drive*

expellō, perf. expulī; repellō, perf. reppulī

prōdo	prōdere	prōdidī	*I betray*
resistō	resistere	restitī	*I resist*
trādō	trādere	trādidī	*I hand over, hand down*

4th Conjugation

aperiō	aperīre	aperuī	*I open*
dēsiliō	dēsilīre	dēsiluī	*I leap down*
saepiō	saepīre	saepsī	*I enclose*
sentiō	sentīre	sensī	*I feel*
vinciō	vincīre	vinxī	*I bind*
veniō	venīre	vēnī	*I come*

Prepositions

(1) With Accusative

ad, *to, towards, for (the purpose of)*

adversus, *against*

ante, *before, in front of*

apud, *near, at the house of*

circum, *round*

contrā, *against*

extrā, *outside*

in, *into, against, on to*

inter, *between, among*

ob, *on account of, because of*

per, *through, throughout, by means of*

pōne, *behind*

post, *after, behind*

praeter, *along, except*

prope, *near*

propter, *on account of, because of*

super, *above*

trans, *across*

ultrā, *beyond*

(2) With Ablative

ā, ab, *from*

cum, *(in company) with*

dē, *down from, concerning, about*

ex, ē, *out of, from, of (after a number)*

in, *in, on, over, among*

prō, *on behalf of, for, in return for, instead of*

sine, *without*

sub, *under*

Latin-English Vocabulary

Verbs which are followed by 1 or 2 or 4, to show the number of their Conjugation, are conjugated regularly in the Perfect Tense.

Proper Nouns are usually not given, if they are the same in English as in Latin.

The long quantity of the final -o *of Verbs has been omitted.*

Ā, ab (with Abl.), *from.*

abstineo, 2 (with ab and Abl.), *I spare.*

absum, -esse, abfuī, *I am away, absent, distant.*

ācer, ācris, ācre, *keen, fierce.*

aciēs, aciēī (f.), *line of battle.*

ad (with Acc.), *to, towards, for (the purpose of).*

addo, -ere, addidī, *I add.*

adhibeo, 2, *I apply.*

adhūc, *still.*

adiuvo, -āre, adiūvī, *help.*

administro, 1, *I govern, manage.*

admīrātiō, -ōnis (f.), *astonishment, admiration.*

admitto, -ere, admīsī, *I let in.*

adōro, 1, *I worship.*

adsum, -esse, adfuī, *I am present, close at hand.*

advena, -ae (c.), *foreigner, stranger.*

adventus, -ūs (m.), *arrival.*

adversus (with Acc.), *against;* adversus clīvum, *uphill.*

aedifico, 1, *I build.*

aeger, aegra, aegrum, *sick, ill.*

aegrōto, 1, *I am ill.*

Aenēās, Aenēae (m.), *Aeneas.*

aēneus, -a, -um, *of bronze.*

āes, āeris (n.), *copper, money.*

aestās, aestātis (f.), *summer.*

ager, agrī (m.), *field, territory.*

agmen, agminis (n.), *column (of soldiers).*

ago, -ere, ēgī, *I drive.*

agricola, -ae (m.), *farmer.*

āla, -ae (f.), *wing, wing of cavalry.*

alacer, alacris, alacre, *active, eager.*

Albānus, -a, -um, *Alban, of Alba;* Albānus, -ī (m.), *an Alban.*

albus, -a, -um, *white.*

Alexander, Alexandrī (m.), *Alexander.*

aliquamdiū, *for some time.*

aliquot, *some.*

altus, -a, -um, *high, deep.*

ambō, ambae, ambō, *both.*

ambulo, 1, *I walk.*

amīcitia, -ae (f.), *friendship.*

amīcus, -ī (m.), *friend.*

amo, 1, *I love, like.*

amor, amōris (m.), *love.*

amphora, -ae (f.), *wine-jar.*

Anchīsēs, Anchīsae (m.), *Anchises.*

ancilla, -ae (f.), *maidservant.*

animal, animālis (n.), *animal.*

animus, -ī (m.), *mind, wits, heart, courage.*

annus, -ī (m.), *year.*

anser, anseris (m.), *goose.*

ante (with Acc.), *before, in front of.*

antīquus, -a, -um, *ancient.*

antrum, -ī (n.), *cave.*

ānulus, -ī (m.), *ring.*

aperio, -īre, aperuī, *I open.*

appāreo, 2, *I appear;* appāret (used impersonally), *it appears.*

appello, 1, *I call (by name).*

appropinquo, 1 (intrans.), *I approach, come near.*

apto, 1 (trans.), *I fit.*

apud (with Acc.), *near, at the house of.*

aqua, -ae (f.), *water.*

āra, -ae (f.), *altar.*

Argīvus, -a, -um, *of Argos;* Argīvī, -ōrum (m. pl.), *the Argives, men of Argos.*

arma, -ōrum (n. pl.), *arms, weapons.*

armātus, -a, -um, *armed.*

armilla, -ae (f.), *bracelet.*

armo, 1, *I arm.*

aro, 1, *I plough.*

arx, arcis (f.), *citadel.*

ascendo, -ere, ascendī, *I climb.*

asper, aspera, asperum, *rough.*

Athēnae, -ārum (f. pl.), *Athens.*

atrox, Gen. atrōcis, *cruel.*

audax, Gen. audācis, *bold.*

audeo, -ēre, *I dare.*

audio, 4, *I hear.*

augeo, -ēre, auxī (trans.), *I increase.*

aureus, -a, -um, *golden.*

aurīga, -ae (c.), *charioteer, driver.*

auris, auris (f.), *ear.*

aurum, -ī (n.), *gold.*

aut, *or;* aut . . . aut, *either . . . or.*

auxilium, -ī (n.), *help.*

avāritia, -ae (f.), *greed.*

Balneae, -ārum (f. pl.), *baths.*

barbarus, -a, -um, *foreign;* barbarī, -ōrum (m. pl.), *barbarians, natives.*

bellum, -ī (n.), *war.*

bene, *well.*

beneficium, -ī (n.), *benefit, good service.*

benevolentia, -ae (f.), *kindness.*

bestia, -ae (f.), *beast.*

blandus, -a, -um, *coaxing.*

Bodotria, -ae (f.), *Firth of Forth.*

bonus, -a, -um, *good;* bona, -ōrum (n. pl.), *goods.*

bōs, bovis (c.), *ox, cow.*

Boudicca, -ae (f.), *Boadicea.*

bracchium, -ī (n.), *arm.*

brevis, breve, *short.*

Britannia, -ae (f.), *Britain.*

Britannus, -ī (m.), *a Briton.*

Cado, -ere, cecidī, *I fall.*

caelum, -ī (n.), *sky.*

Caesar, Caesaris (m.), *Caesar.*

calcar, calcāris (n.), *spur.*

Calēdonia, -ae (f.), *Caledonia, Highlands of Scotland.*

campus, -ī (m.), *plain, field;* **Campus Martius,** *Plain of Mars,* a plain by the Tiber, used for games and military parades.

Camulodūnum, -ī (n.), *Colchester.*

canis, canis (c.), *dog.*

Capitōlium, -ī (n.), *the Capitol.*

captīvus, -ī (m.), *prisoner.*

caput, capitis (n.), *head.*

Caratacus, -ī (m.), *Caractacus.*

carmen, carminis (n.), *song, poem.*

Carthāgō, Carthāginis (f.), *Carthage.*

casa, -ae (f.), *cottage.*

castrum, -ī (n.), *fort;* **castra, -ōrum** (n. pl.), *camp.*

cāsus, -ūs (m.), *fall.*

catēna, -ae (f.), *chain.*

cauda, -ae (f.), *tail.*

causa, -ae (f.), *reason, cause;* **causā** (after Gen.), *for the sake of.*

caveo, -ēre, cāvī, *I am on my guard* (*against*).

caverna, -ae (f.), *cave.*

celeber, celebris, celebre, *famous.*

celebro, 1, *I celebrate, praise.*

celer, celeris, celere, *quick.*

cēlo, 1 (trans.), *I hide.*

cēna, -ae (f.), *dinner, supper.*

cēno, 1, *I dine.*

certo, 1, *I contend, strive, fight.*

certus, -a, -um, *fixed.*

cēterī, -ae, -a, *the rest.*

cibus, -ī (m.), *food.*

Cicerō, Cicerōnis (m.), *Cicero.*

circum (with Acc.), *round.*

circumdo, -are, circumdedī, *I surround.*

circumspecto, 1, *I look round at.*

circumsto, -āre, circumstetī, *I stand round.*

Circus Maximus, *large circus* at Rome for chariot races, etc.

cīvis, cīvis (c.), *citizen.*

cīvitās, -tātis (f.), *state.*

clādēs, clādis (f.), *disaster.*

clam, *secretly.*

clāmo, 1, *I shout, cry out.*

clāmor, clāmōris (m.), *shout.*

clangor, clangōris (m.), *noise of geese, flapping* or *hissing.*

Clānoventa, -ae (f.), *Ravenglass,* in Cumberland.

clārus, -a, -um, *clear.*

claustra, -ōrum (n. pl,), *bars, bolts.*

clāva, -ae (f.), *club.*

clīvus, -ī (m.), *slope, hill.*

cloāca, -ae (f.), *drain, sewer.*

Clōta, -ae (f.), *river Clyde.*

cōgito, 1 (trans), *I think of.*

colloco, 1, *I establish, station.*

colloquium, -ī (n.), *conference.*

colōnia, -ae (f.), *colony, settlement.*

comes, comitis (c.), *companion.*

comminus, *at close quarters, hand to hand.*

committo, -ere, commīsī, proelium, *I join battle.*

commūnico, 1, *I share.*

comparo, 1, *I obtain.*

comporto, 1, *I collect.*

concilio, 1, *I win over.*

concilium, -ī (n.), *council.*

concurro, -ere, concurrī, *I run together.*

confirmo, 1, *I strengthen, encourage, establish.*

congero, -ere, congessī, *I heap.*

coniux, coniugis (c.), *wife, husband.*

consecro, 1, *I dedicate.*

conservo, 1, *I keep safe, preserve.*

consilium, -ī (n.), *plan, advice.*

constituo, -ere, constituī, *I determine.*

consul, consulis (m.), *consul.*

contendo, -ere, contendī, *I march.*

continuus, -a, -um, *continuous.*

contrā (with Acc.), *against.*

cōnūbium, -ī (n.), *intermarriage.*

converto, -ere, convertī (trans.), *I turn.*

convoco, 1, *I call together.*

cōpia, -ae (f.), *plenty;* cōpiae, -ārum (f. pl.), *forces, troops.*

cornū, cornūs (n.), *horn, wing (of army).*

corōno, 1, *I crown.*

corpus, corporis (n.), *body.*

cotīdiānus, -a, -um, *daily.*

cotīdiē, *every day.*

crās, *tomorrow.*

crēdo, -ere, crēdidī (with Dat.), *I believe.*

cremo, 1 (trans.), *I burn.*

cruor, cruōris (m.), *blood.*

crūs, crūris (n.), *leg.*

cubīle, cubīlis (n.), *couch.*

culpo, 1, *I blame.*

cum (with Abl.), *in company with.*

cunīculus, -ī (m.), *tunnel.*

cūr? *why?*

cūra, -ae (f.), *care.*

cūria, -ae (f.), *senate-house.*

cūro, 1, *I look after.*

custōdia, -ae (f.), *confinement, custody.*

custōdio, 4, *I guard.*

custōs, custōdis (c.), *guard.*

Damno, 1, *I condemn.*

dē (with Abl.), *down from, about.*

dea, -ae (f.), *goddess.*

dēbeo, 2 (with Infin.), *I ought.*

dēcerno, -ere, dēcrēvī, *I decide.*

dēcurro, -ere, dēcucurrī or dēcurrī, *I run down.*

dēditiō, -ōnis (f.), *surrender.*

dēdo, -ere, dēdidī, *I give up.*

dēdūco, -ere, dēduxī, *I lead down.*

dēfessus, -a, -um, *tired out.*

deīnde, *then, next.*

dēlecto, 1, *I delight, please.*

dēlectus, -a, -um, *chosen.*

dēleo, -ēre, dēlēvī, *I destroy.*

dēmonstro, 1, *I show, prove.*

dēmulceo, -ēre, dēmulsī, *I lick.*

dēnique, *at last.*

densus, -a, -um, *thick.*

dēseco, -āre, dēsecuī, *I cut off.*

dēsertus, -a, -um, *deserted;* locus dēsertus, *a desert.*

dēsīdero, 1, *I miss.*

dēsilio, -īre, dēsiluī, *I leap down.*

dēsisto, -ere, dēstitī, *I cease;* dēsisto ab, *I cease from.*

dēspēro, 1, *I despair.*

dēturbo, 1, *I throw down, knock down.*

deus, deī (m.), *god.*

Dēva, -ae (f.), *Chester.*

dēvoro, 1, *I devour.*

dexter, dextra, dextrum, *right;* dextra, -ae (f.), *right hand;* ā dextrā, *on the right.*

dictātor, -tōris (m.), *dictator.*

diēs, diēī (m.), *day.*

digitus, -ī (m.), *finger.*

dīrus, -a, -um, *awful, terrible.*

discēdo, -ere, discessī, *depart.*

disco, -ere, didicī, *I learn.*

displiceo, 2 (with Dat.), *I displease.*

diū, *for a long time.*

dīves, Gen. dīvitis, *rich.*

dīvido, -ere, dīvīsī, *I divide.*

do, dare, dedī, *I give.*

doceo, 2, *I teach.*

domicilium, -ī (n.), *home, abode.*

domina, -ae (f.), *mistress (of household).*

dominus, -ī (m.), *master (of household, etc.).*

dōnum, -ī (n.), *gift.*

dormio, 4, *I sleep.*

dormīto, 1, *I fall asleep.*

Druidae, -ārum (m. pl.), *Druids.*

Dubrae, -ārum (f. pl.), *Dover.*

dūco, -ere, duxī, *I lead.*

dum, *while.*

duo, duae, duo, *two.*

dux, ducis (c.), *leader.*

Ē, ex (with Abl.), *out of, from, of* (after a number).

ego, *I.*

elephantus, -ī (m.), *elephant.*

ēligo, -ere, ēlēgī, *I choose.*

ēlūdo, -ere, ēlūsī, *I elude, deceive.*

enim, *for.*

epistola, -ae (f.), *letter.*

epulae, -ārum (f. pl.), *feast, feasts.*

eques, equitis (m.), *horseman;* equitēs, *cavalry.*

equester, equestris, equestre, *of cavalry, cavalry.*

equus, -ī (m.), *horse.*

erro, 1, *I wander.*

esseda, -ae (f.), *war-chariot.*

et, *and, also, even;* et . . . et, *both . . . and.*

etiam, *also, even.*

Etruscī, -ōrum (m. pl.), *the Etruscans.*

ēvādo, -ere, ēvāsī, *I come out, escape.*

ēvoco, 1, *I call out, call forth.*

ēvolo, 1, *I spring forth.*

ex, see ē.

exaudio, 4, *I overhear.*

excito, 1, *I rouse, awake.*

exclāmo, 1, *I shout out.*

exerceo, 2 (trans.), *I train, exercise.*

exercitus, -ūs (m.), *army.*

exitium, -ī (n.), *destruction.*

expello, -ere, expulī, *I drive out.*

explōro, 1, *I spy out, examine, reconnoitre.*

expōno, -ere, exposuī (trans.), *I disembark.*

exspecto, 1, *I wait for, expect.*

exspīro, 1, *I die.*

exsulto, 1, *I exult, boast.*

extrā (with Acc.), *outside.*

Faber, fabrī (m.), *smith, workman.*

fābula, -ae (f.), *story.*

facilis, facile, *easy.*

Faliscī, -ōrum (m. pl.), *the Falisci.*

fatīgo, 1 (trans.), *I tire.*

fēlix, Gen. **fēlīcis**, *fortunate.*

fēmina, -ae (f.), *woman.*

fera, -ae (f.), *wild beast.*

ferē, *almost.*

ferox, Gen. **ferōcis**, *fierce, spirited.*

ferrum, -ī (n.), *iron, sword.*

fessus, -a, -um, *tired.*

festīno, 1, *I hurry.*

fidēs, fideī (f.), *faith, loyalty, pledge, good faith.*

fīlia, -ae (f.), *daughter.*

fīlius, -ī (m.), *son.*

fīnis, fīnis (m.), *end;* **fīnēs** (pl.), *territories, borders.*

fīnitimī, ōrum (m.), *neighbours.*

flāgitium, -ī (n.), *disgraceful act.*

flāgito, 1, *I demand.*

flamma, -ae (f.), *flame.*

flōs, flōris (m.), *flower.*

flūmen, flūminis (n.), *river.*

fluvius, -ī (m.), *river.*

foedus, foederis (n.), *treaty.*

fons, fontis (*m.*), *fountain, spring.*

forte, *by chance.*

fortis, forte, *brave.*

fortūna, -ae (f.), *fortune.*

forum, -ī (n.), *market-place.*

fossa, -ae (f.), *ditch.*

fragor, fragōris (m.), *crash.*

frāter, frātris (m.), *brother.*

frons, frontis (f.), *front.*

frūmentum, -ī (n.), *corn.*

frustrā, *in vain.*

fuga, -ae (f.), *flight, escape.*

fugo, 1, *I rout.*

fulgeo, -ēre, fulsī, *I shine.*

fundo, -ere, fūdī, *I pour.*

Gādēs, -ium (f. pl.), *Cadiz.*

galea, -ae (f.), *helmet.*

Gallia, -ae (f.), *Gaul, France.*

Gallicus, -a, -um, *of the Gauls.*

gallīna, -ae (f.), *hen.*

Gallus, -ī (m.), *a Gaul.*

gero, -ere, gessī, *I carry, wage (war).*

gladius, -ī (m.), *sword.*

Glēvum, -ī (n.), *Gloucester.*

globus, -ī (m.), *band.*

glōria, -ae (f.), *renown.*

Graecia, -ae (f.), *Greece.*

Graecus, -a, -um, *Greek;* **Graecus, -ī**, *a Greek.*

grātiam habeo, *I feel thankful.*

grātus, -a, -um, *pleasing, welcome.*

grex, gregis (m.), *flock, herd.*

guberno, 1, *I steer.*

Gȳgēs, Gȳgis (m.), *Gyges.*

Habeo, 2, *I have, hold, consider.*

habito, 1 (trans.), *I inhabit;* (intrans.), *I live, dwell.*

Hadria, -ae (m.), *Adriatic Sea.*

haereo, -ēre, haesī (intrans.), *I stick.*

Hannibal, -balis (m.), *Hannibal.*

hasta, -ae (f.), *spear.*

herba, -ae (f.), *grass.*

Herculēs, -is (m.), *Hercules.*

hērōs, hērōis (m.), *hero.*

Hibernia, -ae (f.), *Ireland.*

hīc, *here.*

hiemo, 1, *I spend the winter.*

hiems, hiemis (f.), *winter.*

hinc ... hinc, *on this side ... on that side.*

hio, 1, *I gape, lie open.*

hodiē, *today.*

Homērus, -ī (m.), *Homer.*

homō, hominis (m.), *man (opposed to animal).*

honestus, -a, -um, *honourable.*

honōro, 1, *I honour.*

honōs, honōris (m.), *honour.*

hōra, -ae (f.), *hour.*

hospes, hospitis (m.), *guest, host, friend.*

hospitium, -ī (n.), *hospitality.*

hostis, hostis (c.), *enemy (public).*

hūmānus, -a, -um, *human.*

Iaceo, 2, *I lie.*

iacto, 1, *I hurl.*

iam, *already, now;* nōn iam, *no longer.*

iānua, -ae (f.), *door.*

ibi, *there.*

igitur, *therefore.*

ignis, ignis (m.), *fire.*

ignōro, 1, *I do not know.*

imber, imbris (m.), *shower.*

immolo, 1, *I sacrifice.*

impedio, 4, *I hinder.*

imperātor, -tōris (m.), *general, commander.*

imperium, -ī (n.), *power, sway.*

impero, 1, *I command.*

impetus, -ūs (m.), *attack, rush.*

impleo, -ēre, implēvī, *I fill.*

importo, 1, *I import.*

in (with Acc.), *into, against, on to.*

in (with Abl.), *in, on, over, among.*

incautus, -a, -um, *unwary.*

incēdo, -ere, incessī, *I advance.*

incito, 1, *I rouse, encourage.*

incola, -ae (c.), *native, inhabitant.*

incompositus, -a, -um, *in disorder.*

inde, *thence, then, from that time.*

Indī, -ōrum (m. pl.), *the Indians.*

indico, 1, *I show, betray.*

Indicus, -a, -um, *Indian.*

inermis, inerme, *unarmed.*

infestus, -a, -um, *hostile.*

ingens, Gen. ingentis, *huge.*

inimīcus, -ī (m.), *enemy (private).*

inīquus, -a, -um, *uneven.*

iniustus, -a, -um, *unjust.*

inopia, -ae (f.), *want, scarcity.*

inops, Gen. inopis, *helpless.*

inquit, *he says;* inquiunt, *they say.*

insideo, -ēre, insēdī, *I sit on.*

insidiae, -ārum (f. pl.), *ambush.*

insignis, insigne, *famous, conspicuous.*

instituo, -ere, instituī, *I begin.*

insto, -āre, institī, *I threaten.*

insula, -ae (f.), *island.*

intellego, -ere, intellexī, *I understand.*

inter (with Acc.), *between, among.*

interdum, *sometimes.*

interim, *meanwhile.*

intermitto, -ere, intermīsī, *I leave off, interrupt.*

intervallum, -ī (n.), *distance.*

intro, 1, *I enter.*

invenio, -īre, invēnī, *I find.*

invicem, *in turn.*

invideo, -ēre, invīdī (with Dat.), *I envy, begrudge.*

invīto, 1, *I invite.*

īra, -ae (f.), *anger.*

īrātus, -a, -um, *angry.*

is, ea, id, *this, that; he, she, it.*

ita, *in this way, so.*

Ītalia, -ae (f.), *Italy.*

itaque, *therefore.*

iter, itineris (n.), *journey.*

iterum, *again.*

iubeo, -ēre, iussī, *I order.*

Iūnō, Iūnōnis (f.), *Juno.*

Iuppiter, Iovis (m.), *Jupiter.*

iūro, -āre, iūrāvī, *I swear.*

iūs, iūris (n.), *right.*

iussū, *by order.*

iustitia, -ae (f.), *justice.*

iustus, -a, -um, *just.*

iuvenis, iuvenis (c.), *young man, young woman.*

iuvo, -āre, iūvī, *I help.*

Labefacto, 1, *I overthrow, destroy.*

labor, labōris (m.), *work.*

labōro, 1 (intrans.), *I work.*

laetus, -a, -um, *joyful, glad.*

laevus, -a, -um, *left.*

latebrae, -ārum (f. pl.), *hiding-place.*

lateo, 2, *I lie hid.*

Latīnus, proper name; Latīnus, -a, -um, *Latin.*

latrō, latrōnis (m.), *robber.*

latus, lateris (n.), *side.*

lātus, -a, -um, *broad, wide.*

laudo, 1, *I praise.*

Laurentīnus, -a, -um, *of Laurentum,* a town on the coast of Latium.

lēgātus, -ī (m.), *ambassador.*

legiō, legiōnis (f.), *legion.*

lego, -ere, lēgī, *I read.*

leō, leōnis (m.), *lion.*

levo, 1, *I lift.*

lex, lēgis (f.), *law.*

liber, librī (m.), *book.*

līber, lībera, līberum, *free.*

līberī, -ōrum (m. pl.), *children.*

lībero, 1, *I free.*

Lindum, -ī (n.), *Lincoln.*

lingua, -ae (f.), *tongue, language.*

linter, lintris (f.), *boat.*

loco, 1, *I place.*

locus, -ī (m.), *place.*

Londīnium, -ī (n.), *London.*

longinquus, -a, -um, *distant.*

longus, -a, -um, *long.*

lōrīca, -ae (f.), *breastplate.*

lūcet (impersonal Verb of 2nd Conjug.), *it is light.*

lūdus, -ī (m.), *game.*

lūna, -ae (f.), *moon.*

luxuria, -ae (f.), *luxury.*

Lȳdia, -ae (f.), *Lydia.*

Lȳdus, -ī (m.), *a Lydian.*

Maestus, -a, -um, *sad.*

magister, magistrī (m.), *master (of school).*

magistrātus, -ūs (m.), *magistrate.*

magnus, -a, -um, *great, large, loud.*

mando, 1, *I entrust.*

māne, *in the morning.*

maneo, -ēre, mansī, *I remain, stay.*

manus, -ūs (f.), *hand, band (of men).*

mare, maris (n.), *sea.*

mātrimōnium, -ī (n.), *marriage.*

mātūrus, -a, -um, *ripe.*

maximus, -a, -um, *very big.*

medicīna, -ae (f.), *healing, remedy.*

medicus, -ī (m.), *doctor.*

Melita, -ae (f.), *Malta.*

membrum, -ī (n.), *limb.*

memor, Gen. **memoris,** *mindful.*

mensa, -ae (f.), *table.*

merīdiānus, -a, -um, *of noon.*

merīdiēs, merīdiēī (m.), *noon.*

meus, -a, -um, *my, mine.*

migro, 1, *I migrate, move.*

mīles, mīlitis (c.), *soldier.*

ministro, 1, *I serve out.*

mīrāculum, -ī (n.), *wonder.*

mīrus, -a, -um, *wonderful, strange.*

mītigo, 1, *I soften.*

mitto, -ere, mīsī, *I send.*

modo, *only;* **nōn modo . . . sed etiam,** *not only . . . but also;* **modo . . . modo,** *at one time . . . at another time.*

modus, -ī (m.), *way, method, means.*

mōmentum, -ī (n.), *moment.*

Mona, -ae (f.), *Anglesey.*

moneo, 2, *I advise, warn.*

mons, montis (m.), *mountain.*

monstro, 1, *I show.*

mora, -ae (f.), *delay.*

moribundus, -a, -um, *dying.*

mortuus, -a, -um, *dead.*

mōs, mōris (m.), *custom.*

moveo, -ēre, mōvī (trans.), *I move, start (war).*

mox, *soon.*

mulco, 1, *I beat.*

mulier, mulieris (f.), *woman.*

multitūdō, -dinis (f.), *crowd, great number.*

multus, -a, -um, *much* (in pl. *many);* **multum,** *much, far.*

mūnio, 4, *I fortify, build (road).*

mūnus, mūneris (n.), *gift.*

murmur, murmuris (n.), *roar.*

mūrus, -ī (m.), *wall.*

mūsica, -ae (f.), *music.*

Narro, 1, *I tell, recount.*

nato, 1, *I swim.*

nātūra, -ae (f.), *nature.*

nauta, -ae (m.), *sailor.*

nāvicula, -ae (f.), *little boat.*

nāvigo, 1 (intrans.), *I sail.*

nāvis, nāvis (f.), *ship.*

-ne? (at the end of a word denotes a question).

nē . . . quidem, *not even.*

nebula, -ae (f.), *mist.*

nec, neque, *and not, nor;* **nec . . . nec, neque . . . neque,** *neither . . . nor;* **nec tamen,** *but . . . not* neco, 1, *I kill.*

neglego, -ere, neglexī, *I neglect.*

nēmō, Acc. nēminem (no Gen. or Abl.), *no one.*

neque, see nec.

niger, nigra, nigrum, *black.*

nihil, *nothing.*

nimbus, -ī (m.), *rain-cloud.*

nisi, *unless, if not, except.*

noctū, *by night.*

nōlo, *I am unwilling;* nōlī, nōlīte (imperative, followed by infinitive), *do not.*

nōmen, nōminis (n.), *name.*

nōn, *not;* nōn iam, *no longer.*

nonne? *not* in question of which the expected answer is *yes.*

nōnus, -a, -um, *ninth.*

noster, nostra, nostrum, *our.*

noto, 1, *I observe, note.*

nōtus, -a, -um, *well-known.*

novus, -a, -um, *new, strange.*

nox, noctis (f.), *night.*

nūbēs, nūbis (f.), *cloud.*

nullus, -a, -um, *no, none.*

num? *surely not* in question of which the answer is already felt to be *no.*

numerus, -ī (m.), *number.*

nunc, *now.*

nuntio, 1, *I announce.*

Ō (exclamation sometimes used with Vocative), *O.*

ob (with Acc.), *on account of, because of.*

obsecro, 1, *I beseech.*

obses, obsidis (c.), *hostage.*

obstinātus, -a, -um, *steadfast, resolute.*

obtineo, 2, *I hold.*

occīdo, -ere, occīdī, *I kill.*

occumbo, -ere, occubuī, *I die.*

occupo, 1, *I seize.*

oculus, -ī (m.), *eye.*

oleum, -ī (n.), *oil.*

omnīnō, *altogether.*

omnis, omne, *all, every.*

onus, oneris (n.), *burden.*

oppidum, -ī (n.), *town.*

opprimo, -ere, oppressī, *I overwhelm.*

oppugno, 1, *I attack.*

opus, operis (n.), *work.*

ōra, -ae (f.), *shore.*

ōrātor, ōrātōris (m.), *spokesman.*

ornāmentum, -ī (n.), *trappings.*

orno, 1, *I equip.*

ōro, 1, *I beg, beg for, pray.*

ostento, 1, *I display.*

ovis, ovis (f.), *sheep.*

Paene, *almost.*

pāla, -ae (f.), *bezel* (part of ring in which stone is set).

palma, -ae (f.), *palm (of hand).*

palūs, palūdis (f.), *marsh.*

paluster, palustris, palustre, *marshy.*

parātus, -a, -um, *ready.*

parens, parentis (c.), *parent.*

pāreo, 2 (with Dat.), *I obey.*

paro, 1, *I prepare.*

pars, partis (f.), *part; some.*

parumper, *for a short time.*

parvus, -a, -um, *small.*

passim, *in all directions.*
pateo, 2, *I lie open.*
pater, patris (m.), *father.*
patria, -ae (f.), *country, native land.*
paucī, -ae, -a, *few.*
paulātim, *gradually.*
pauper, Gen. pauperis, *poor.*
paveo, -ēre, pāvī, *I quake with fear.*
pavor, pavōris (m.), *panic.*
pax, pācis (f.), *peace.*
pecūnia, -ae (f.), *money.*
pedes, peditis (m.), *foot-soldier;* peditēs, *infantry.*
penetro, 1, *I penetrate.*
per (with Acc.), *through, throughout, by means of, by* (in an oath).
perequito, 1, *I drive about.*
perfuga, -ae (m.), *fugitive, deserter.*
perīculum, -ī (n.), *danger.*
Persae, -ārum (m. pl.), *the Persians.*
perturbo, 1, *I throw into confusion.*
pervenio, -īre, pervēnī (intrans.), *I arrive;* pervenio ad (with Acc.), *I reach.*
pēs, pedis (m.), *foot.*
peto, -ere, petīvī, *I seek, make for.*
placeo, 2 (with Dat.), *I please;* placet (used impersonally), *it pleases.*
placidus, -a, -um, *gentle.*
plaga, -ae (f.), *net, trap.*
plēnus, -a, um, *full.*

plōrātus, -ūs (m.), *wailing.*
pluvia, -ae (f.), *rain.*
poena, -ae (f.), *punishment.*
Pompēius, -ī (m.), *Pompey.*
pōmum, -ī (n.), *apple.*
pondus, ponderis (n.), *weight.*
pōne (with Acc.), *behind.*
pōno, -ere, posuī, *I place.*
pons, pontis (m.), *bridge.*
populus, -ī (m.), *people.*
porta, -ae (f.), *gate.*
porto, 1, *I carry.*
post (with Acc.), *after, behind.*
posteā, *afterwards.*
posterī, -ōrum (m. pl.), *descendants.*
postulo, 1, *I demand.*
potestās, -tātis (f.), *power.*
potius, *rather.*
pōto, 1, *I drink.*
praebeo, 2, *I offer, furnish.*
praecipito, 1, *I hurl headlong.*
praeclārus, -a, -um, *famous.*
praecō, praecōnis (m.), *herald.*
praeda, -ae (f.), *booty.*
praedō, praedōnis (m.), *robber, pirate.*
praefectus, -ī (m.), *commander, governor.*
praemium, -ī (n.), *reward.*
praesidium, -ī (n.), *garrison.*
praesto, -āre, praestitī, *I offer, give.*
praesum, -esse, praefuī (with Dat.), *I am in command of.*
praeter (with Acc.), *along, except.*
praetōrium, -ī (n.), *general's tent.*

primō, prīmum, *first, at first.*

prīmus, -a, -um, *first.*

princeps, principis (c.), *chief.*

prō (with Abl.), *on behalf of, for, in return for, instead of.*

prōcēdo, -ere, prōcessī, *I go forward, advance.*

procella, -ae (f.), *storm.*

procul, *far.*

prōditiō, -ōnis (f.), *treachery.*

prōditor, -tōris (m.), *traitor.*

prōdo, -ere, prōdidī, *I betray.*

proelium, -ī (n.), *battle.*

prōmitto, -ere, prōmīsī, *I promise.*

prope (with Acc.), *near;* (Adverb) *almost.*

propero, 1, *I hurry.*

propinquus, -ī (m.), *relative.*

propter (with Acc.), *on account of, because of.*

prōpulso, 1, *I drive back.*

prosper, prospera, prosperum, *prosperous.*

prōvideo, -ēre, prōvīdī, *I foresee.*

prōvincia, -ae (f.), *province.*

prōvoco, 1, *I challenge.*

proximus, -a, -um, *next.*

prūdentia, -ae (f.), *foresight.*

puella, -ae (f.), *girl.*

puer, puerī (m.), *boy.*

pugna, -ae (f.), *fight, battle.*

pugno, 1 (intrans.), *I fight.*

pulcher, pulchra, pulchrum, *beautiful.*

Quam, *than.*

quanquam, *although.*

quartus, -a, -um, *fourth.*

quattuor, *four.*

quō?, *whither?*

quod, *because.*

quondam, *once (upon a time).*

quoque, *also.*

quot?, *how many?*

Recens, Gen. recentis, *fresh.*

recenseo, 2, *I review.*

recipero, 1 (trans.), *I recover.*

recūso, 1, *I refuse.*

redigo, -ere, redēgī, *I reduce.*

redūcō, -ere, reduxī, *I lead back.*

reformīdo, 1, *I dread.*

rēgīna, -ae (f.), *queen.*

rēgius, -a, -um, *royal.*

regno, 1, *I reign.*

regnum, -ī (n.), *kingdom.*

rego, -ere, rexī, *I rule.*

relinquo, -ere, relīquī, *I leave behind, abandon.*

reliquus, -a, -um, *remaining;* in pl., *the rest.*

remitto, -ere, remīsī, *I send back.*

remōtus, -a, -um, *distant, retired.*

removeo, -ēre, remōvī (trans.), *I remove, withdraw.*

repello, -ere, reppulī, *I drive back.*

repente, *suddenly.*

reporto, 1, *I carry back, bring back, win (a victory).*

repudio, 1, *I reject, refuse.*

requiesco, -ere, requiēvī, *I rest.*

rēs, reī (f.), *thing, event, affair.*

resisto, -ere, restitī (with Dat.). *I resist.*

resono, 1, *I echo.*

respondeo, -ēre, respondī, *I reply.*

rēspublica, reīpublicae (f.), *state, commonwealth.*

restituo, -ere, restituī, *I restore.*

retineo, 2, *I keep, detain.*

retrō, *backwards.*

revello, -ere, revellī, *I pull away.*

revoco, 1, *I call back.*

rex, rēgis (m.), *king.*

Rhēnus, -ī (m.), *the Rhine.*

rīdeo, -ēre, rīsī, *I laugh.*

rīpa, -ae (f.), *bank.*

rogo, 1, *I ask, ask for.*

Rōma, -ae (f.), *Rome.*

Rōmānī, -ōrum (m. pl.), *the Romans.*

Rōmānus, -a, -um, *Roman.*

rota, -ae (f.), *wheel.*

ruīna, -ae (f.), *fall.*

rumpo, -ere, rūpī (trans.), *I break.*

rursus, *again.*

rūs, rūris (n.), *country* (opposed to *town*).

Sabīnī, -ōrum (m. pl.), *the Sabines.*

Sabrīna, -ae (f.), *the Severn.*

sacer, sacra, sacrum, *sacred.*

sacerdōs, -dōtis (m.), *priest.*

sacrificō, 1, *I sacrifice.*

saepe, *often.*

saepio, -īre, saepsī, *I enclose.*

saevus, -a, -um, *savage.*

sagitta, -ae (f.), *arrow.*

salūber, salūbris, salūbre, *healthy.*

salūto, 1, *I greet.*

salvus, -a, -um, *safe, unhurt.*

sanguis, sanguinis (m.), *blood, bloodshed.*

sāno, 1, *I cure.*

sapiens, Gen. sapientis, *wise.*

sapientia, -ae (f.), *wisdom.*

satis, *enough;* with Gen., *enough of.*

saucius, -a, um, *wounded.*

saxum, -ī (n.), *rock.*

scelestus, -a, -um, *wicked, villainous.*

scelus, sceleris (n.), *crime.*

scrībo, -ere, scripsī, *I write.*

scūtum, -ī (n.), *shield.*

sē (reflexive Pronoun), *himself, herself, itself, themselves.*

seco, -āre, secuī, *I cut.*

secundus, -a, -um, *second.*

sed, *but.*

sedeo, -ēre, sēdī, *I sit.*

semper, *always.*

senātus, -ūs (m.), *senate.*

senex, senis (m.), *old man.*

sententia, -ae (f.), *opinion.*

sentio, -īre, sensī, *I perceive, feel.*

sēparo, 1, *I separate.*

septem, *seven.*

septimus, -a, -um, *seventh.*

sermō, sermōnis (m.), *conversation, discourse.*

servus, -ī (m.), *slave, servant.*

sex, *six.*

sextus, -a, -um, *sixth.*

sī, *if.*

sīc, *so, thus.*

sicco, 1 (trans.), *I dry.*

Sicilia, -ae (f.), *Sicily.*

signum, -ī (n.), *sign, signal*.

silentium, -ī (n.), *silence*.

silva, -ae (f.), *wood*.

similis, simile (with Gen.), *like*.

sine (with Abl.), *without*.

sinister, sinistra, sinistrum, *left;* sinistra, -ae (f.), *left hand;* ā sinistrā, *on the left*.

socer, socerī (m.), *father-in-law*.

societās, -tātis (f.), *alliance*.

socius, -ī (m.), *ally*.

Sōcratēs, -is (m.), *Socrates*.

sōl, sōlis (m.), *sun*.

soleo, -ēre, *I am accustomed*.

solitus, -a, -um, *usual, accustomed*.

solium, -ī (n.), *throne*.

sōlum, *only*.

sono, -āre, sonuī, *I sound*.

spatium, -ī (n.), *interval*.

spectāculum, -ī (n.), *show, sight*.

specto, 1, *I watch, look at;* specto ad (with Acc.), *I look towards, face*.

spēlunca, -ae (f.), *cave*.

spēro, 1, *I hope, hope for*.

spēs, speī (f.), *hope*.

spīna, -ae (f.), *thorn*.

statim, *at once*.

statiō, statiōnis (f.), *outpost*.

statua, -ae (f.), *statue*.

stella, -ae (f.), *star*.

sto, stāre, stetī, *I stand*.

strangulo, 1, *I strangle*.

sub (with Abl.), *under*.

subitō, *suddenly*.

sublevo, 1, *I lift up*.

sublicius, -a, -um, *built on piles*.

sum, esse, fuī, *I am*.

super (with Acc.), *above*.

supero, 1, *I conquer*.

supersum, -esse, superfuī, *I am left over, survive*.

suppedito, 1, *I provide, supply*.

sūs, suis (c.), *pig*.

sustineo, 2, *I endure, bear*.

suus, -a, -um (reflexive Adjective), *his, her, its, their, own*.

Taberna, -ae (f.), *shop*.

taceo, 2, *I am silent*.

tacitus, -a, -um, *silent*.

taeda, -ae (f.), *torch*.

tam (with Adjective), *so*.

tamen, *however*.

tandem, *at last*.

tantus, -a, -um, *so great*.

tardo, 1, *I delay*.

Tarquiniī, -ōrum (m. pl.), *the Tarquins*.

Tarquinius Priscus, *Tarquin the Elder*.

taurus, -ī (m.), *bull*.

tego, -ere, texī, *I cover*.

tēlum, -ī (n.), *weapon*.

tempestās, -tātis (f.), *storm*.

templum, -ī (n.), *temple*.

tempto, 1, *I try, attempt*.

tempus, temporis (n.), *time*.

teneo, 2, *I hold*.

tergum, -ī (n.), *back;* ā tergō, *in the rear*.

terra, -ae (f.), *land, earth, country*.

terreo, 2, *I frighten*.

terror, terrōris (m.), *fright*.

tertius, -a, -um, *third*.

theātrum, -ī (n.) *theatre.*

Thessalia, -ae (f.), *Thessaly.*

Thrācia, -ae (f.), *Thrace.*

Tiberīnus, -a, -um, *of the Tiber.*

Tiberis, Tiberis (m.), *the Tiber.*

timeo, 2, *I fear, am afraid (of).*

tolero, 1, *I put up with, endure.*

tot, *so many.*

tōtus, -a, -um, *whole.*

tracto, 1, *I tug, haul.*

trādo, -ere, trādidī, *I hand over.*

traho, -ere, traxī, *I drag.*

trāno, 1, *I swim across.*

trans (with Acc.), *across.*

transporto, 1, *I carry across.*

trepido, 1, *I am in a panic, bustle about.*

trepidus, -a, -um, *alarmed.*

trēs, tria, *three.*

Trōia, -ae (f.), *Troy.*

Trōiānī, -ōrum (m. pl.), *the Trojans.*

trucīdo, 1, *I butcher.*

tū, *you* (sing.).

tum, *then.*

turba, -ae (f.), *crowd.*

turma, -ae (f.), *squadron (of cavalry).*

turpis, turpe, *disgraceful, shameful.*

tūtus, -a, -um, *safe.*

tuus, -a, -um, *your* (sing.).

Ubi, *when, where.*

ubi? *where?*

ubīque, *everywhere.*

ultrā (with Acc.), *beyond.*

umbra, -ae (f.), *shade.*

ūnā, *together.*

unda, -ae (f.), *wave.*

undecim, *eleven.*

undique, *on all sides.*

ungula, -ae (f.), *hoof.*

ūnus, -a, -um, *one.*

urbs, urbis (f.), *city.*

usque ad (with Acc.), *as far as, right up to.*

ut, *as, when.*

ūtilis, ūtile, *useful.*

Vacca, -ae (f.), *cow.*

vacuus, -a, -um, *empty.*

vādo, -ere, *I go, stride.*

valeo, 2, *I avail, am strong.*

validus, -a, -um, *strong.*

vallum, -ī (n.), *rampart.*

vario, 1, *I vary, change.*

vasto, 1, *I lay waste, ravage.*

vectigal, vectīgālis (n.), *tax.*

Vēiens, Gen. Vēientis, *of Veii.*

venēnum, -ī (n.), *poison.*

venia, -ae (f.), *pardon.*

venio, -īre, vēnī, *I come.*

verber, verberis (n.), *lash.*

verbero, 1, *I beat.*

verbum, -ī (n.), *word.*

verto, -ere, vertī (trans.), *I turn.*

Verulāmium, -ī (n.), *St. Albans.*

vesper, vesperī (m.), *evening.*

vester, vestra, vestrum, *your* (pl.).

vestīgium, -ī (n.), *track.*

vetus, Gen. veteris, *old.*

vexo, 1, *I distress.*

via, -ae (f.), *way, road.*

victōria, -ae (f.), *victory.*

video, -ēre, vīdī, *I see.*

vigilo, 1, *I am awake.*

villa, -ae (f.), *country-house, farm.*

vincio, -īre, vinxī, *I bind.*

vinco, -ere, vīcī, *I conquer, overcome.*

vīnum, -ī (n.), *wine.*

violentia, -ae (f.), *violence.*

vir, virī (m.), *man* (opposed to
woman), *husband.*

virga, -ae (f.), *rod.*

virgō, virginis (f.), *maiden.*

Vīrocōnium, -ī (n.), *Wroxeter* (in
Shropshire).

virtūs, -tūtis (f.), *courage.*

vīs (f.), *force, violence* (see Summary of Grammar for its declension); vīrēs, vīrium (f. pl.),
strength.

vīta, -ae (f.), *life.*

vīto, 1, *I avoid, shun.*

vīvo, -ere, vīxī, *I live.*

vix, *scarcely, with difficulty.*

voco, 1, *I call.*

volo, 1, *I fly.*

vox, vōcis (f.), *voice.*

vulnero, 1, *I wound.*

vulnus, vulneris (n.), *wound.*

English-Latin Vocabulary

Verbs which are followed by 1 or 2 or 4, to show the number of their Conjugation, are conjugated regularly in the Perfect Tense.

Proper Nouns are usually not given, if they are the same in Latin as in English.

The long quantity of the final -o *of Verbs has been omitted.*

About (*concerning*), **dē** (with Abl.); *about* (*number*), **ferē**.

account of, on, **ob, propter** (with Acc.).

accustomed, I am, **soleo, -ēre**.

across, **trans** (with Acc.).

active, **alacer, alacris, alacre**.

admiration, **admīrātiō, -ōnis** (f.).

Adriatic, **Hadria, -ae** (m.).

advance, I, **prōcēdo, -ere, prōcessī; incēdo, -ere, incessī**.

advice, **consilium, -ī** (n.).

advise, I, **moneo, 2**.

Aeneas, **Aenēās, Aenēae** (m.).

afraid, I am, **timeo** (2); *afraid of, I am,* **timeo** (with Acc.).

after, **post** (with Acc.).

afterwards, **posteā**.

again, **rursus, iterum**.

against, **contrā, adversus** (with Acc.).

Alban, **Albānus, -a, -um;** *an Alban,* **Albānus, -ī** (m.).

Alexander, **Alexander, Alexandrī** (m.).

all, **omnis, omne**.

alliance, **societās, -tātis** (f.).

ally, **socius, -ī** (m.).

almost, **paene**.

alone, **sōlus, -a, -um**.

along, **praeter** (with Acc.).

already, **iam**.

also, **etiam**.

altar, **āra, -ae** (f.).

although, **quanquam**.

always, **semper**.

am, I, **sum, esse, fuī**.

ambassador, **lēgātus, -ī** (m.).

ambush, **insidiae, -ārum** (f. pl.).

among, **inter** (with Acc.).

Anchises, **Anchīsēs, Anchīsae** (m.).

anchor, **ancora, -ae** (f.).

ancient, **antīquus, -a, -um**.

and, **et, ac** (before consonant), **atque;** *and not,* **nec, neque**.

anger, **īra, -ae** (f.).

Anglesey, **Mona, -ae** (f.).

angry, **īrātus, -a, -um**.

animal, **animal, animālis** (n.).

announce, I, **nuntio, 1**.

appear, I, **appāreo, 2**.

apple, **pōmum, -ī** (n.).

approach, I, **appropinquo, 1** (intrans., with **ad** and Acc.).

Argives, the, **Argīvī, -ōrum** (m. pl.).

arm (*of body*), **bracchium, -ī** (n.).

arm, I, **armo, 1.**

arms (*weapons*), **arma, -ōrum** (n. pl.).

army, **exercitus, -ūs** (m.).

arouse, I, **excito, 1.**

arrive at, I, **pervenio, -īre, pervēnī, ad** (with Acc.).

as, **ut.**

as far as, **usque ad** (with Acc.).

ascend, I, **ascendo, -ere, ascendī.**

ask, ask for, I, **rogo, 1.**

at once, **statim.**

Athens, **Athēnae, -ārum** (f. pl.).

attack, I, **oppugno, 1.**

attack, **impetus, -ūs** (m.).

attempt, I, **tempto, 1.**

awake, I (trans.), **excito, 1.**

awake, I am, **vigilo, 1.**

Back, **tergum, -ī** (n.).

backwards, **retrō.**

band, **manus, -ūs** (f.).

bank, **rīpa, -ae** (f.).

banquet, **epulae, -ārum** (f. pl.).

barbarian, a, **barbarus, -ī** (m.).

baths, **balneae, -ārum** (f. pl.).

battle, **pugna, -ae** (f.); **proelium, -ī** (n.).

beat, I (*hit*), **mulco, 1.**

beautiful, **pulcher, pulchra, pulchrum.**

because, **quod.**

because of, **ob, propter** (with Acc.).

before (Prep.), **ante** (with Acc.); (Advb. *in the past*), **anteā.**

beg (*for*), *I,* **ōro.**

behalf of, on, **prō** (with Abl.).

belief, **fidēs, fideī** (f.).

besides, **praetereā.**

besiege, I, **obsideo, -ēre, obsēdī.**

between, **inter** (with Acc.).

beyond, **ultrā** (with Acc.).

big, **magnus, -a, -um;** *very big,* **maximus, -a, -um.**

blame, I, **culpo, 1.**

blood-stained, **cruentus, -a, -um.**

Boadicea, **Boudicca, -ae** (f.).

boat, little, **nāvicula, -ae** (f.).

body, **corpus, -oris** (n.).

bold, **audax,** Gen. **audācis.**

boldness, **audācia, -ae** (f.).

book, **liber, librī** (m.).

booty, **praeda, -ae** (f.).

both, **ambō, ambae, ambō;** *both . . . and,* **et . . . et.**

boy, **puer, puerī** (m.).

brave, **fortis, forte.**

bravery, **fortitūdō, -dinis** (f.).

break, break down, I, **rumpo, -ere, rūpī.**

breastplate, **lōrīca, -ae** (f.).

bridge, **pons, pontis** (m.).

Britain, **Britannia, -ae** (f.).

Britons, the, **Britannī, -ōrum** (m. pl.).

broad, **lātus, -a, -um.**

bronze, of, **aēneus, -a, -um.**

brother, **frāter, frātris** (m.).

Bucephalas, **Būcephalās, -ae** (m.).

build, I, **aedifico, 1.**

building, **aedificium, -ī** (n.).

burden, **onus, oneris** (n.).

burn, I (trans.), **cremō, 1.**

but, **sed;** *but . . . not,* **nec tamen.**

butcher, I, **trucīdo, 1.**

Caesar, Caesar, Caesaris (m.).

call, *I*, voco, 1; *call back*, *I*, revoco, 1; *call together*, *I*, convoco, 1.

call by name, *I*, appello, 1.

camp, castra, -ōrum (n. pl.).

Capitol, Capitōlium, -ī (n.).

Capri, Capreae, -ārum (f. pl.).

Caractacus, Caratacus, -ī (m.).

carry, *I*, porto, 1; *carry across*, *I*, transporto, 1.

Carthage, Carthāgō, Carthāginis (f.).

cause, causa, -ae (f.).

cavalry, equitēs, -um (m. pl.); *cavalry*, *of cavalry* (adj.), equester, equestris, equestre.

cavalry squadron, turma, -ae (f.).

cave, spēlunca, -ae (f.); caverna, -ae (f.); antrum, -ī (n.).

cease, *I*, dēsisto, -ere, dēstitī; *cease from*, *I*, dēsisto ab (with Abl.).

celebrated, celeber, celebris, celebre.

chain, catēna, -ae (f.).

chance, by, forte.

chariot, esseda, -ae (f.).

Charles, Carolus, -ī (m.).

Chester, Dēva, -ae (f.).

chicken, gallīna, -ae (f.).

chief (Noun), princeps, principis (c.); (Adj.), princeps, Gen. principis.

children, līberī, -ōrum (m.pl.).

choose, *I*, ēligo, -ere, ēlēgī.

Christians, Christiānī, -ōrum (m. pl.).

circus, circus, -ī (m.).

citadel, arx, arcis (f.).

citizen, cīvis, cīvis (c.).

city, urbs, urbis (f.).

clear, clārus, -a, -um.

clever, doctus, -a, -um.

climb, *I*, supero, 1; ascendo, -ere, ascendī.

cloud, nūbēs, nūbis (f.).

club, clāva, -ae (f.).

Clyde, the, Clōta, -ae (f.).

coast, ōra, -ae (f.).

Colchester, Camulodūnum, -ī (n.)

cold, frīgus, frīgoris (n.).

colony, colōnia, -ae (f.).

come near, *I*, appropinquo, 1 (intrans.).

command, *I*, impero, 1; iubeo, -ēre, iussī.

commander, praefectus, -ī (m.).

companion, comes, comitis (c.).

conquer, *I*, supero, 1; vinco, -ere, vīcī.

consent, consensus, -ūs (m.).

conspicuous, insignis, -e.

consul, consul, consulis (m.).

copper, āes, āeris (n.).

corn, frūmentum, -ī (n).

cottage, casa, -ae (f.).

country, a, terra, -ae (f.); (*native land*), patria, -ae (f.); (opposed to *town*), rūs, rūris (n.).

country-house, villa, -ae (f.).

courage, virtūs, -tūtis (f.).

cover, *I*, tego, -ere, texī.

cow, vacca, -ae (f.).

crash, fragor, fragōris (m.).

crowd, turba, -ae (f.).

cruel, atrox, Gen. atrōcis.

cry out, *I*, clāmo, 1 ; exclāmo, 1.

cut, *I*, seco, -āre, secuī.

Danger, perīculum, -ī (n.).

dare, *I*, audeo, -ēre.

darken, *I* (trans.), obscūro, 1 .

daughter, fīlia, -ae (f.).

day, diēs, diēī (m.).

dead, mortuus, -a, -um.

dear, cārus, -a, -um.

death, mors, mortis (f.).

decide, *I*, constituo, -ere, constituī.

dedicate, *I*, consecro, 1.

deed, rēs, reī (f.).

defeat, *I*, supero, 1 ; vinco, -ere, vīcī.

defend, *I*, dēfendo, -ere, dēfendī.

delay, *I* (trans.), tardo, 1.

delay, mora, -ae (f.).

delight, *I* (trans.), dēlecto, 1.

demand, *I*, postulo, 1 ; flāgito, 1.

depart, *I*, discēdo, -ere, discessī.

desert, locus desertus (m.).

deserter, perfuga, -ae (m.).

despair, *I*, dēspēro, 1.

destroy, *I*, dēleo, -ēre, dēlēvī.

destruction, exitium, -ī (n.).

determine, *I*, constituo, -ere, constituī.

devour, *I*, dēvoro, 1.

dictator, dictātor, -tōris (m.).

difficult, difficilis, difficile.

dine, *I*, cēno, 1.

dinner, cēna, -ae (f.).

directions, *in all*, passim.

disembark, *I* (trans.), expōno, -ere, exposuī.

disgraceful, turpis, turpe.

display, *I*, ostento, 1.

distant, longinquus, -a, -um.

ditch, fossa, -ae (f.).

doctor, medicus, -ī (m.).

dog, canis, canis (c.).

Domitian, Domitiānus, -ī (m.).

door, iānua, -ae (f.).

Dover, Dubrae, -ārum (f. pl.).

drag, *I*, traho, -ere, traxī.

draw up, *I*, instruo, -ere, instruxī.

dread, *I*, reformīdo, 1.

drive, *I*, pello, -ere, pepulī; *drive back*, *I*, prōpulso, 1; repello, -ere, reppulī; *drive out*, *I*, expello, -ere, expulī.

drive about, *I* (intrans.), perequito, 1.

Druids, Druidae, -ārum (m. pl.)

Each other, inter sē.

eager, alacer, alacris, alacre.

eagle, aquila, -ae (f.).

earth, terra, -ae (f.).

easy, facilis, facile.

either . . . or, aut . . . aut.

elect, *I*, creo, 1.

enclose, *I*, saepio, -īre, saepsī.

encourage, *I*, confirmo, 1.

endure, *I*, sustineo, 2.

enemy (*of country*), hostis, hostis (c.), mostly used in pl. for *the enemy; private enemy*, inimīcus, -ī (m.).

enter, *I*, intro, 1.

entrust, *I*, mando, 1.

envy, invidia, -ae (f.).

establish, I (*a colony*), **colloco**, 1;
(*friendship, alliance, etc.*), **con-firmo**, 1.

Etruscans, the, **Etruscī, -ōrum** (m. pl.).

even, **etiam.**

examine, I, **explōro,** 1.

example, **exemplum, -ī** (n.).

except, **praeter** (with Acc.); *after a negative,* **nisi.**

exercise, I, **exerceo,** 2.

expect, I, **exspecto,** 1.

eye, **oculus, -ī** (m.).

Face, I, **specto,** 1 (with **ad** and Acc.).

faith, **fidēs, fideī** (f.).

faithless, **perfidus, -a, -um.**

Falerii, **Falērii, -ōrum** (m. pl.).

fall, I, **cado, -ere, cecidī.**

fall asleep, **dormīto,** 1.

famous, **celeber, celebris, celebre.**

far (*from*), **procul** (ab, with Abl.); *far from, I am,* **multum absum ab.**

farmer, **agricola, -ae** (m.).

father, **pater, patris** (m.).

fear, I, **timeo,** 2.

feel, I, **sentio, -īre, sensī.**

feel grateful, I, **grātiam habeo.**

few, **paucī, -ae, -a.**

field, **ager, agrī** (m.); *field of Mars,* **Campus Martius.**

fierce, **saevus, -a, -um;** (*of war*), use **ācer.**

fight, I (intrans.), **pugno,** 1.

fight, **pugna, -ae** (f.).

fill, I, **impleo, -ēre, implēvī.**

finally, **postrēmō.**

find, I, **invenio, -īre, invēnī.**

finger, **digitus, -ī** (m.).

fire, **ignis, ignis** (m.).

fire, I am on, **ardeo, -ēre, arsī.**

first, **prīmus, -a, -um;** *at first,* **prīmum.**

five, **quinque.**

flame, **flamma, -ae** (f.).

flight, **fuga, -ae** (f.).

flock, **grex, gregis** (m.).

flower, **flōs, flōris** (m.).

fly, I, **volo,** 1; *fly out, I,* **ēvolo,** 1.

food, **cibus, -ī** (m.).

foolish, **stultus, -a, -um.**

foot, **pēs, pedis** (m.).

for (conjunction), **nam** (1st word); **enim** (2nd word).

for (*on behalf of*), **prō** (with Abl.); but often, Dative of Advantage.

for (*the purpose of*), **ad** (with Acc.).

for the sake of, **causā** (after Gen.).

force, **vīs** (f.): see Summary of Grammar for its declension.

forced march, **magnum iter, magnī itineris** (n.).

forces, **cōpiae, -ārum** (f. pl.).

foreigner, **advena, -ae** (c.).

fort, **castellum, -ī** (n.).

Forth, Firth of, **Bodotria, -ae** (f.).

fortify, I, **mūnio,** 4.

fortunate, **fēlix,** Gen. **fēlīcis.**

fortune, **fortūna, -ae** (f.).

fountain, **fons, fontis** (m.).

four, **quattuor.**

fourth, quartus, -a, -um.

France, Gallia, -ae (f.).

free, I, libero, 1.

free, liber, libera, liberum.

freedom, libertās, -tātis (f.).

fresh, recens, Gen. recentis.

friend, amicus, -i (m.).

friendship, amicitia, -ae (f.).

frighten, I, terreo, 2.

from, ā, ab before a vowel (with Abl.); ē, ex before a vowel (with Abl.); *from there*, inde; *from where?* unde?

full, plēnus, -a, -um.

Game, lūdus, -i (m.).

garden, hortus, -i (m.).

garrison, praesidium, -i (n.).

gate, porta, -ae (f.).

Gaul, Gallia, -ae (f.); *a Gaul*, Gallus, -i (m.).

general, imperātor, -tōris (m.).

gentle, placidus, -a, -um.

gift, dōnum, -i (n.).

girl, puella, -ae (f.).

give, I, dō, dare, dedi; *give up, I*, dēdo, -ere, dēdidī.

glad, laetus, -a, -um.

go away, I, discēdo, -ere, discessī; *go into, I*, intro, 1.

god, deus, -i (m.).

goddess, dea, -ae (f.).

gold, aurum, -i (n.).

golden, aureus, -a, -um.

good, bonus, -a, -um.

goods, bona, -ōrum (n. pl.).

good service, beneficium, -i (n.).

goose, anser, anseris (m.).

governor, praefectus, -i (m.).

grass, herba, -ae (f.).

grateful, I am (*feel*), grātiam habeo.

great, magnus, -a, -um; *so great*, tantus, -a, -um.

Greece, Graecia, -ae (f.).

greed, avāritia, -ae (f.).

Greek, a, Graecus, -i (m.).

greet, I, salūto, 1.

ground, locus, -i (m.); *on the ground*, humī (Locative).

guard, I, custōdio, 4; *guard against, I*, caveo, -ēre, cāvī.

guard, custōs, custōdis (c.).

guest, hospes, hospitis (m.).

Gyges, Gȳgēs, Gȳgis (m.).

Hand, manus, -ūs (f.).

hand down, I, trādo, -ere, trādidī; *hand over, I*, trādo; dēdo, -ere, dēdidī.

harm, I, noceo, 2 (with Dat.).

hasten, I, propero, 1; festīno, 1.

have, I, habeo, 2.

hay, herba, -ae (f.).

he, is.

head, caput, capitis (n.).

healthy, salūber, salūbris, salūbre.

heap, I, congero, -ere, congessī.

hear, I, audio, 4.

helmet, galea, -ae (f.).

help, I, iuvo, -āre, iūvī.

help, auxilium, -i (n.).

helpless, inops, Gen. inopis.

hen, gallīna, -ae (f.).

her (*own*, reflexive), suus, -a, -um.

Hercules, Herculēs, -is (m.).

here, hīc; *here, I am,* adsum, -esse, adfuī.

hesitate, I, dubito, 1.

hide, I (trans.), cēlo, 1.

high, altus, -a, -um.

hill, clīvus, -ī (m.).

hinder, I, impedio, 4.

his, ēius; *his own* (reflexive), suus, -a, -um.

hold, I, teneo, 2; *hold back, I,* retineo, 2.

home (abode), domicilium, -ī (n.); domus, -ūs or -ī (f.); *at home,* domī; *homewards,* domum.

honourable, honestus, -a, -um.

hope, hope for, I, spēro, 1.

hope, spēs, speī (f.).

horse, equus, -ī (m.).

hospitality, hospitium, -ī (n.).

host, hospes, hospitis (m.).

hostage, obses, obsidis (c.).

hour, hōra, -ae (f.).

house, domus, -ūs or -ī (f.); *country-house,* villa, -ae (f.).

how many? quot?

however, tamen (2nd word).

huge, ingens, Gen. ingentis.

human, hūmānus, -a, -um.

hurl headlong, I, praecipito, 1.

hurry, I, propero, 1; festīno, 1.

hut, casa, -ae (f.).

I, ego.

if, sī.

ill, aeger, aegra, aegrum.

import, I, importo, 1.

in, in (with Abl.).

incautiously, use Adj. incautus, -a, -um.

increase, I (trans.), augeo, –ēre, auxī.

India, India, -ae (f.).

Indians, the, Indī, -ōrum (m. pl.).

infantry, peditēs, -um (m. pl.).

inhabitant, incola, -ae (c.).

instead of, prō (with Abl.).

into, in (with Acc.).

invite, I, invīto, 1.

Ireland, Hibernia, -ae (f.).

island, insula, -ae (f.).

Italy, Ītalia, -ae (f.).

Journey, via, -ae (f.); iter, itineris (n.).

jump down, I, dēsilio, -īre, dēsiluī.

Juno, Iūno, Iūnōnis (f.).

Jupiter, Iuppiter, Iovis (m.).

just, iustus, -a, -um.

justice, iustitia, -ae (f.).

Keep, keep safe, I, conservo, 1.

kill, I, neco, 1; occīdo, -ere, occīdī.

kindness, benevolentia, -ae (f.).

king, rex, rēgis (m.).

kingdom, regnum, -ī (n.).

knee, genū, -ūs (n.).

know, I, scio, 4; *how to,* with Infin.

know, I do not, ignōro, 1.

Lady, mātrōna, -ae (f.).

lair, latebrae, -ārum (f. pl.).

land, terra, -ae (f.); *native land,* patria, -ae (f.).

language, lingua, -ae (f.).

large, magnus, -a, -um.

lash, verber, verberis (n.).

last, at, tandem.

laugh, I, rīdeo, -ēre, rīsī.

lay waste, I, vasto, 1.

lead, I, dūco, -ere, duxī; *lead away, I*, abdūco.

leader, dux, ducis (c.).

learn, I, disco, -ere, didicī.

leave, I, relinquo, -ere, relīquī.

left, sinister, sinistra, sinistrum; *left hand*, sinistra, -ae (f.); *on the left*, ā sinistrā.

left, I am, supersum, -esse, super-fuī.

legion, legiō, legiōnis (f.).

length, at, tandem.

Leonidas, Leōnidās, Leōnidae (m.).

let in, I, admitto, -ere, admīsī.

letter, epistola, -ae (f.).

lick, I, dēmulceo, -ēre, dēmulsī.

lie, I, iaceo, 2.

life, vīta, -ae (f.).

lift, lift up, I, levo, 1.

like, I, amo, 1.

line of battle, aciēs, aciēī (f.).

lion, leō, leōnis (m.).

little, parvus, -a, -um.

live (dwell) in, I, habito, 1, in (with Abl.); *(am alive)*, vīvo, -ere, vixī.

Livy, Līvius, -ī (m.).

London, Londīnium, -ī (n.).

long, longus, -a, -um.

long time, for a, diū.

longer, no, nōn iam.

look after, I, cūro, 1.

look at, I, specto, 1; *look towards I*, specto ad (with Acc.).

loud, magnus, -a, -um.

love, I, amo, 1.

Lydia, Lȳdia, -ae (f.).

Lydian, a, Lȳdus, -ī (m.).

Macedonians, Macedonēs, -um (m.).

maid, maid-servant, ancilla, -ae (f.)

magistrate, magistrātus, -ūs (m.).

maiden, virgō, virginis (f.).

make for, I, peto, -ere, petīvī.

man (opposed to woman), vir, virī (m.); *(opposed to animal)*, homō, hominis (m.).

many, see much.

marriage, mātrimōnium, -ī (n.); *marriage, I give in*, in mātri-mōnium do.

marshy, paluster, palustris, pal-ustre.

master (of household, etc.), dominus, -ī (m.).

master (of school), magister, magistrī (m.).

means of, by, per (with Acc.).

meanwhile, interim.

memory, memoria, -ae (f.).

messenger, nuntius, -ī (m.).

mid-day (Adj.), merīdiānus, -a, -um.

mist, nebula, -ae (f.).

mistress (of household), domina, -ae (f.).

moderation, modestia, -ae (f.).

moment, mōmentum, -ī (n.), tem-poris.

money, pecūnia, -ae (f.).

moon, lūna, -ae (f.).

morning, in the, māne.

mountain, mons, montis (m.).

much, multus, -a, -um; *many*, multī, -ae, -a.

my, meus, -a, -um (Voc. m. sing. mī).

Name, nōmen, nōminis (n.).

native, incola, -ae (c.).

native land, patria, -ae (f.).

native (Adj.), patrius, -a, -um.

nature, nātūra, -ae (f.).

near, prope (with Acc.).

nearly, prope.

neglect, I, neglego, -ere, neglexī.

neither . . . nor, nec . . . nec; neque . . . neque.

net, plaga, -ae (f.).

never, nunquam.

new, novus, -a, -um.

next, proximus, -a, -um.

next day, on the, postrīdiē.

night, nox, noctis (f.); *by night*, noctū.

ninth, nōnus, -a, -um.

no longer, nōn iam.

no one, nēmō, Acc. nēminem (no Gen. or Abl.).

nor, nec; neque.

not, nōn; *not even*, nē . . . quidem; *not* in question of which the expected answer is *yes*, nonne?

not only . . . but also, nōn modo . . . sed etiam.

not yet, nōndum.

nothing, nihil.

now, nunc, iam.

Obey, I, pāreo, 2 (with Dat.).

obtain, I, comparo, 1.

offer, I, praesto, -āre, praestitī; praebeo, 2.

often, saepe.

oil, oleum, -ī (n.).

old man, senex, senis (m.).

on, in (with Abl.).

on horseback, I fight, ex equō pugno.

on to, in (with Acc.).

once (upon a time), quondam, ōlim.

once, at, statim.

one, ūnus, -a, -um.

only, modo.

open, I, aperio, -īre, aperuī.

opinion, sententia, -ae (f.).

or, aut.

order, I, impero, 1; iubeo, -ēre, iussī.

others, the, cēterī, -ae, -a.

our, noster, nostra, nostrum; *our men*, nostrī.

out of, ē, ex before a vowel (with Abl.).

outpost, statiō, statiōnis (f.).

outside, extrā (with Acc.).

overcome, I, supero, 1.

overhear, I, exaudio, 4.

overthrow, I, dēturbo, 1.

owing to, ob, propter (with Acc.).

Pardon, venia, -ae (f.).

parent, parens, parentis (c.).

part, pars, partis (f.).

pass, angustiae, -ārum (f. pl.).

peace, pax, pācis (f.).

penetrate, I, penetro, 1.

people, populus, -ī (m.).

perhaps, fortasse.

Persians, the, Persae, -ārum (m. pl.).

pile (Adj.), sublicius, -a, -um.

place, I, pōno, -ere, posuī.

place, locus, -ī (m.).

plain, campus, -ī (m.).

plan, consilium, -ī (n.).

playing-field, campus, -ī (m.).

pleasant, iūcundus, -a, -um.

please, I, dēlecto, 1 ; placeo, 2 (with Dat.).

pledge, fidēs, fideī (f.).

plenty, cōpia, -ae (f.).

plough, I, aro, 1.

plunder, I, vasto, 1.

point out, I, monstro, 1.

poison, venēnum, -ī (n.).

poor, pauper, Gen. pauperis.

position, locus, -ī (m.).

power, imperium, -ī (n.).

praise, I, laudo, 1.

prepare, I, paro, 1.

pretend, I, simulo, 1.

priest, sacerdōs, -dōtis (m.).

prince, rēgulus, -ī (m.).

prisoner, captīvus, -ī (m.).

promise, I, prōmitto, -ere, prōmīsī.

provide, I, praebeo, 2.

province, prōvincia, -ae (f.).

Queen, rēgīna, -ae (f.).

Race (*human*), genus, generis (n.).

rain, pluvia, -ae (f.).

rain-cloud, nimbus, -ī (m.).

rampart, vallum, -ī (n.).

rank, ordō, ordinis (m.).

rather, potius.

ravage, I, vasto, 1.

Ravenglass, Clānoventa, -ae (f.).

reach, I, pervenio, -īre, pervēnī, ad (with Acc.).

read, I, lego, -ere, lēgī.

recall, I, revoco, 1.

recognise, I, noscito, 1.

reconnoitre, I, explōro, 1.

reign, I, regno, 1.

reject, I, repudio, 1.

relate, I, narro, 1.

relation, propinquus, -ī (m.).

remain, I, maneo, -ēre, mansī.

remaining (Adj.), reliquus, -a, -um.

remove, I (trans.), removeo, -ēre, remōvī.

renown, glōria, -ae (f.).

reply, I, respondeo, -ēre, respondī.

return for, in, prō (with Abl.).

review, I, recenseo, 2.

reward, praemium, -ī (n.).

Rhine, the, Rhēnus, -ī (m.).

Rhone, the, Rhodanus, -ī (m.).

rich, dīves, Gen. dīvitis.

right, dexter, dextra, dextrum; *right hand*, dextra, -ae (f.) ; *on the right*, ā dextrā.

ring, ānulus, -ī (m.).

ripe, mātūrus, -a, -um.

river, fluvius, -ī (m.); flūmen, flūminis (n.).

road, via, -ae (f.).

roar, murmur, murmuris (n.).

roast, I, torreo, 2.

robber, latrō, latrōnis (m.).

rock, saxum, -ī (n.).

Roman, Rōmānus, -a, -um; *Romans, the*, Rōmānī, -ōrum (m. pl.).

Rome, Rōma, -ae (f.).

rough, asper, aspera, asperum.

rouse, I, excito, 1.

rout, I, fugo, 1.

royal, rēgius, -a, -um.

rule, I, rego, -ere, rexī.

run, I, curro, -ere, cucurrī.

Sabines, the, Sabīnī, -ōrum (m. pl.).

sacred, sacer, sacra, sacrum.

sacrifice, I, sacrifico, 1.

sad, tristis, triste.

safe, tūtus, -a, -um; salvus, -a, -um.

safety, salūs, salūtis (f.).

sail, I (intrans.), nāvigo, 1.

sailor, nauta, -ae (m.).

sake of, for the, causā (after Gen.).

save, I, conservo, 1.

says he, inquit; *they say*, inquiunt.

scarcity, inopia, -ae (f.).

school, lūdus, -ī (m.).

schoolmaster, magister, magistrī (m.).

Scotland, Calēdonia, -ae (f.).

scout, explōrātor, -tōris (m.).

sea, mare, maris (n.).

second, secundus, -a, -um.

secretly, clam.

see, I, video, -ēre, vīdī.

seek, I, peto, -ere, petīvī.

seize, I, occupo, 1.

senate, senātus, -ūs (m.).

senators, patrēs, patrum (m. pl.).

send, I, mitto, -ere, mīsī; *send back*, I, remitto, -ere, remīsī.

service, good, beneficium, -ī (n.).

set free, I, lībero, 1.

settlement, colōnia, -ae (f.).

seven, septem.

Severn, the, Sabrīna, -ae (f.).

shade, umbra, -ae (f.).

sharp, ācer, ācris, ācre.

shield, scūtum, -ī (n.).

ship, nāvis, nāvis (f.).

shop, taberna, -ae (f.).

shore, ōra, -ae (f.).

short, brevis, breve.

shout, I, clāmo, 1; *shout out*, I, exclāmo, 1.

shout, clāmor, clāmōris (m.).

show, I, monstro, 1.

show, spectāculum, -ī (n.).

Sicily, Sicilia, -ae (f.).

sick, aeger, aegra, aegrum.

sides, on all, passim.

sight, spectāculum, -ī (n.).

signal, signum, -ī (n.).

Silchester, Callēva, -ae (f.).

silent, I am, taceo, 2.

sing, I, canto, 1; cano, -ere, cecinī.

sister, soror, sorōris (f.).

sit, I, sedeo, -ēre, sēdī.

skin, pellis, pellis (f.).

slave, servus, -ī (m.).

sleep, I, dormio, 4.

sleep, somnus, -ī (m.).

slope, clīvus, -ī (m.).

small, parvus, -a, -um.

smile, I, rīdeo, -ēre, rīsī.

so (*thus*), ita, sīc.

so great, tantus, -a, -um.

soldier, mīles, mīlitis (c.).

some, aliquot; *some ..., some ...,* use pars, partis (f.), *part*.

sometimes, interdum.

son, fīlius, -ī (m.).

song, carmen, carminis (n.).

soon, mox.

spare, I, abstineo, 2, ab.

speak, I, dīco, -ere, dixī.

spear, hasta, -ae (f.).

spend the winter, I, hiemo, 1.

spirited, ferox, Gen. ferōcis.

spy out, I, explōro, 1.

St. Albans, Verulāmium, -ī (n.).

stand, I, sto, stāre, stetī.

star, stella, -ae (f.).

start (*a fight, war*), *I*, moveo, -ēre, mōvī (pugnam, bellum).

state, cīvitās, -tātis (f.); rēspublica, reīpublicae (f.).

station, I, colloco, 1.

statue, statua, -ae (f.).

stay, I, maneo, -ēre, mansī.

steel, ferrum, -ī (n.).

step, gradus, -ūs (m.).

stick, I (intrans.), haereo, -ēre, haesī.

still (*yet*), adhūc.

stone, saxum, -ī (n.).

storm, procella, -ae (f.); tempestās, -tātis (f.).

story, fābula, -ae (f.).

strange, novus, -a, -um.

stranger, advena, -ae (c.).

street, via, -ae (f.).

strength, vīrēs, vīrium (f. pl.).

strengthen, I, confirmo, 1.

such, tālis, tāle.

suddenly, subitō; repente.

sun, sōl, sōlis (m.).

supper, I have, cēno, 1.

supper, cēna, -ae (f.).

supply, I, suppedito, 1.

surely ... not? num?

surrender, I (trans.), dēdo, -ere, dēdidī.

surround, I, circumdo, -are, circumdedī.

swim, I, nato, 1.

swim, across, I, trāno, 1.

sword, gladius, -ī (m.).

Tail, cauda, -ae (f.).

take by storm, I, expugno, 1.

tax, vectīgal, vectīgālis (n.).

teach, I, doceo, 2.

tell (*a story*), *I*, narro, 1.

temple, templum, -ī (n.).

ten, decem.

tender, tener, tenera, tenerum.

tent(*of general*), praetōrium, -ī (n.).

terrible, dīrus, -a, -um.

territory, ager, agrī (m.).

that, is, ea, id.

theatre, theātrum, -ī (n.).

their, eōrum, eārum, eōrum; *their own* (reflexive), suus, -a, -um.

themselves (reflexive Pronoun), sē.

then (*next*), dēinde; tum; (*at that time*), tum.

there, ibi; *from there*, inde.

therefore, igitur (2nd word).

Thermopylae, Thermopylae, -ārum (f. pl.).

thick, densus, -a, -um.

think of, *I*, cōgito, 1 (with Acc.).

third, tertius, -a, -um.

this, is, ea, id.

three, trēs, tria.

throne, solium, -ī (n.).

through, *throughout*, per (with Acc.).

throw into confusion, *I*, perturbo, 1.

Tiber, *the*, Tiber, Tiberis (m.).

time, tempus, temporis (n.).

tire, *I* (trans.), fatīgo, 1.

tired, fessus, -a, -um.

to (*towards*), ad (with Acc.).

today, hodiē.

together, ūnā.

tomorrow, crās.

tongue, lingua, -ae (f.).

torch, taeda, -ae (f.).

towards (*place*), ad (with Acc.).

town, oppidum, -ī (n.).

train, *I*, exerceo, 2.

traitor, prōditor, -tōris (m.).

trap, plaga, -ae (f.).

trappings, ornāmentum, -ī (n.).

trick, dolus, -ī (m.).

Trojans, *the*, Trōiānī, -ōrum (m. pl.).

troops, cōpiae, -ārum (f. pl.).

Troy, Trōia, -ae (f.).

truth, use vēra (n. pl. of Adj. vērus, *true*).

tunnel, cunīculus, -ī (m.).

turn round, *I* (intrans.), me converto, -ere, convertī.

two, duo, duae, duo.

Uncle, avunculus, -ī (m.).

under, sub (with Abl.).

understand, *I*, intellego, -ere, intellexī.

unhurt, salvus, -a, -um.

unless, nisi.

urge on, *I*, incito, 1.

useful, ūtilis, ūtile.

Vain, *in*, frustrā.

Veii, Vēiī, -ōrum (m. pl.).

victory, victōria, -ae (f.).

violate, *I*, violo, 1.

voice, vox, vōcis (f.).

Wag, *I*, moveo, -ēre, mōvī.

wage war, *I*, bellum gero, -ere, gessī.

wait for, *I*, exspecto, 1.

walk, *I*, ambulo, 1.

wall, mūrus, -ī (m.).

wander, *I*, erro, 1.

war, bellum, -ī (n.).

warn, *I*, moneo, 2.

watch, *I*, specto, 1.

watch, vigilia, -ae (f.).

water, aqua, -ae (f.).

wave, unda, -ae (f.).

way, via, -ae (f.).

way, *in this*, ita, sīc.

wealth, dīvitiae, -ārum (f. pl.).

weapon, tēlum, -ī (n.).

weary, fessus, -a, -um.

welcome, grātus, -a, -um.

well-known, nōtus, -a, -um.

wheel, rota, -ae (f.).

when, ubi.

where? ubi?

where, from? unde?

where to? quō?

why? cūr?

wicked, malus, -a, -um; scelestus, -a, -um.

wild beast, fera, -ae (f.).

win (victory), I, reporto, 1.

win over, I, concilio, 1.

wine, vīnum, -ī (n.).

wing (of army), cornū, -ūs (n.).

wisdom, sapientia, -ae (f.).

wise, sapiens, Gen. sapientis.

with, in company, cum (with Abl.).

without, sine (with Abl.).

withstand, I, sustineo, 2.

woman, fēmina, -ae (f.); mulier, mulieris (f.).

wonder, mīrāculum, -ī (n.).

wonderful, mirus, -a, -um.

wood, silva, -ae (f.).

word, verbum, -ī (n.).

work, I, laboro, 1.

work (toil), labor, labōris (m.); *(a work),* opus, operis (n.).

workman, faber, fabrī (m.).

worship, I, adōro, 1.

worthy of, dignus, -a, -um (with Abl.).

wound, vulnus, vulneris (n.).

wretched, miser, misera, miserum.

write, I, scrībo, -ere, scripsī.

wrong, wrongdoing, iniūria, -ae (f.).

Xerxes, Xerxēs, Xerxis (m.).

Year, annus, -ī (m.).

yearn for, I, dēsīdero, 1.

you (s.), tū; *you (pl.),* vōs.

young man, iuvenis, iuvenis (m.).

your (s.), tuus, -a, -um; *your (pl.),* vester, vestra, vestrum.

youth, a, iuvenis, iuvenis (m.).

Lists of Commoner Words

These words are all worth learning and remembering for future use. All the meanings should be known, together with all Declensions and Genders of Nouns, Declensions of Adjectives and Pronouns, and Conjugations of Verbs.

The words are arranged under the headings of the chapters in which they first occur in this book.

Most of the words occur in the Latin-English exercises and therefore in the Latin-English general vocabulary; a few occur only in the examples given in the particular chapter. In the very few instances where a common Latin word has only been wanted for use in an English-Latin exercise, the English word is given instead of the Latin; the Latin word will be found in the English-Latin vocabulary. All Proper Nouns and most Numerals have been omitted.

CHAPTER 1

aedifico	despero	nato	pugno
ambulo	erro	navigo	sed
amo	et	nec	sto
aro	exploro	neque	supero
aut	intro	non	vasto
ceno	iuvo	occupo	voco
clamo	laboro	oppugno	volo
culpo	laudo	propero	

CHAPTER 2

agricola	filia	nauta	regina
femina	luna	puella	vacca

CHAPTER 3

aqua	fortuna	ora	silva
celo	habito	paro	specto
curo	herba	pecunia	stella
deinde	insula	porto	tandem
delecto	interdum	postulo	terra
diu	ita	primo	umbra
epistola	mensa	quod	via
exspecto	monstro	saluto	
fera	neco	seco	

CHAPTER 4

conservo	vito	*anchor*

CHAPTER 5

amicitia	hasta	patria	statim
appropinquo	hiemo	perturbo	tamen
comparo	iacto	porta	tum
copia	insidiae	praeda	ubi (*when*)
copiae	insto	primum	ubi? (*where?*)
cur?	libero	pugna	unde?
do	mox	quo?	victoria
excito	-ne?	quot?	vita
fabula	nec tamen	reporto	vulnero
fossa	nonne?	revoco	*goddess*
fugo	num?	sagitta	

CHAPTER 6

ara	fatigo	nuntio	semper
avaritia	ianua	omnino	turba
colloco	ibi	paene	*memory*
colonia	ira	rursus	*wrong*
convoco	natura	saepe	

CHAPTER 7

enim	incito	ostento	transporto
etiam	mando	praesto	venia
galea	narro	taeda	

Chapter 8

a, ab	confirmo	in (with Abl.)	spelunca
aliquot	cum	indico	spero
armo	dextra	latebrae	*eagle*
catena	dum	mora	*I take by*
			storm
circumdo	e, ex	retro	
clam	flamma	si	
concilio	forte	sine	

Chapter 9

ad	interim	praeter	rogo
ante	iustitia	pro	sententia
contra	ob	prope	trans
festino	oro	propter	unda
flagito	per	prudentia	vexo
in (with Acc.)	post	regno	*pass*

Chapter 10

a dextra	epulae	procul	ultra
a sinistra	gloria	provincia	unā
administro	hic	trucido	usque ad
ala	inde	ubi (*where*)	
bene	modo	ubique	

Chapter 11

augeo	igitur	removeo	taceo
de	ignoro	respondeo	teneo
deleo	lingua	rideo	terreo
exerceo	maneo	rota	timeo
fuga	moneo	subito	video
habeo	paulatim	sustineo	*wealth*

CHAPTER 12

adversus	faber	liber	puer
ager	filius	liberi	retineo
amicus	fluvius	locus	servus
barbari	gener	magister	socer
campus	gladius	murus	socius
captivus	iaceo	nunc	tardo
custodia	iam	oculus	vesper
deus	inter	populus	vir
dominus	iuro	propinquus	

CHAPTER 13

arma	doceo	oppidum	saxum
auxilium	humus	pareo	signum
bellum	imperium	periculum	templum
castellum	importo	placeo	vallum
castra	inquit	praefectus	venenum
caveo	moveo	praemium	vinum
certo	noceo	proelium	
consilium	oleum	repudio	

CHAPTER 14

altus	dirus	multus	sedeo
antiquus	invito	nimbus	tuus
appareo	iterum	non iam	ut (*as*)
bonus	magnus	numerus	vacuus
caelum	meus	parvus	*garden*
densus	mirus	regius	

CHAPTER 15

adhuc	dexter	niger	sano
aeger	hodie	noster	sinister
albus	impero	pauci	sinistra
asper	līber	posteri	tener
bona (n. pl.)	longinquus	praebeo	vester
causā	longus	pulcher	*besides*
cogito	miser	sacer	*for* (nam)

o

Chapter 16

aeneus	gratus	notus	sapientia
apto	honestus	novus	sic
aureus	inimicus	palma	solitus
beneficium	itaque	pomum	sum
clarus	laetus	praeclarus	tantus
donum	lātus	praesidium	tutus
equus	maturus	quondam	verbum
fessus	maximus	regnum	*dear*
forum	mortuus	repente	

Chapter 17

absum	colloquium	hospitium	supersum
adsum	comporto	multum (*far*)	tot
barbarus (Adj.)	domicilium	nihil	*envy*
cibus	evoco	olim (*once*)	*I am on fire*

Chapter 18

frumentum	loco	*wicked*

Chapter 19

animus	frustra	mater	saevus
apud	grex	miles	sol
consul	heros	ne ... quidem	valeo
demonstro	homo	nemo	vestigium
denique	impero	pater	virtus
dux	invideo	pedes	vox
eques	lateo	potius	*I elect*
exitium	latro	quam	
frater	leo	rex	

Chapter 20

ceteri	modus	prope (*almost*)	*never*
cras	nisi	spectaculum	*not yet*
impleo	pax	terror	
iustus	placidus	*before* (Advb.)	

CHAPTER 21

aes	cotidianus	murmur	validus
antrum	crus	nomen	verber
apparet	desertus	obtineo	vulnus
appello	flos	onus	*blood-stained*
caput	flumen	opus	*school*
carmen	imperator	pes	*I sing*
causa	iniustus	salvus	
clamor	iratus	sub	
corpus	levo	tergum	

CHAPTER 22

bracchium	ego	poena	*sister*
circum	gratiam habeo	postea	*year*
cruor	haereo	quoque	
damno	hospes	tu	
desidero	membrum	*I roast*	

CHAPTER 23

extra	is	provideo	undique
honos	latus	satis	*native* (Adj.)
incautus	orno	telum	

CHAPTER 24

amor	inopia	proximus	tempto
anser	invicem	reliquus	unus
comes	noctu	ruina	vigilo
custos	pone	se	*foolish*
humanus	praecipito	silentium	*sleep*
iniquus	primus	suus	

CHAPTER 25

canis	ferrum	maestus	rupes
civis	fines	mitto	traho
clades	finitimi	mulier	vinco
coniux	hostis	multitudo	virgo
conubium	ignis	navis	*building*
dedo	imber	nubes	*messenger*
discedo	iuvenis	parens	*I violate*
duco	linter	recuso	
expello	ludus	rego	

CHAPTER 26

animal	fons	peto	scutum
arx	frons (*front*)	pondus	urbs
ascendo	gero	pons	vectigal
aurum	laevus	praedo	*safety*
calcar	mare	praesum	*I speak the truth*
civitas	mons	promitto	*trick*
credo	nox	rumpo	
cubile	opprimo	rus	
disco	ornamentum	scribo	

CHAPTER 27

acer	desisto	munio	venio
addo	equester	palus	verto
alacer	evado	pavor	vivo
aperio	hinc ... hinc	pervenio	vix
audio	impedio	repello	*faithless*
auris	incedo	saluber	
celeber	infestus	tacitus	
celer	invenio	tempestas	

CHAPTER 28

custodio	insignis	proditio	turpis
decurro	obsecro	relinquo	utilis
difficilis	omnis	resisto	vado
facilis	pars	sentio	*cold* (noun)
fortis	pateo	trepidus	*rank*

CHAPTER 29

atrox	dormio	labor	sapiens
audax	felix	neglego	spatium
brevis	ferox	parumper	super
cado	fundo	quanquam	tego
defessus	ingens	recens	*skin*
desilio	intellego	remitto	

CHAPTER 30

adventus	foedus	ludo	reduco
cedo	genu	manus	restituo
cornu	gradus	obses	ripa
deduco	impetus	occīdo	senatus
domus	legatus	pono	*boldness*
exercitus	lego	prodo	

CHAPTER 31

adiuvo	exsulto	procedo	tres
ambo	fulgeo	sanguis	veto
casus	iubeo	saucius	*bravery*
circumsto	legio	solum	*death*
committo	nullus	solus	*finally*
converto	obsideo	sono	*I pretend*
duo	praeco	totus	*sad*

CHAPTER 32

acies	divido	meridies	spes
adhibeo	exaudio	momentum	tempus
agmen	fere	plenus	*I draw up*
ago	fides	potestas	*on the next day*
certus	finis	redigo	*scout*
continuus	hora	res	*watch*
decerno	inermis	respublica	*worthy*
dictator	intermitto	revello	
dies	iussu	sacerdos	

CHAPTER 33

aestas	expono	mos	soleo
audeo	hiems	munus	statio
constituo	immemor	pauper	trado
cotidie	inops	princeps	vetus
cura	instituo	scelus	*I defend*
debeo	intervallum	scio	*freedom*
dives	ius	sermo	
dubito	memor	similis	

CHAPTER 34

bos	iter	senex	*example*
celebro	lex	sus	*forced march*
concilium	magistratus	tam	*pleasant*
concurro	nolo	taurus	*race*
contendo	ovis	vincio	*I run*
curia	paratus	vis	*such*
deditio	placet	*I drive*	

Additional Exercises

EXERCISE 172 (Chapters 1–5)

1. Regina terram vastat.
2. Vacca umbram non vitat.
3. Reginam salutamus.
4. Epistola nautam delectat.
5. Nautae insulam oppugnant.
6. Agricola feras necat.
7. Cenam parate.
8. Nauta stellas spectat.
9. Copiae insulas occupant.
10. Agricola aquam postulat.
11. Portam intramus.
12. Aquae terram celant.
13. Sagittam vita.
14. Victoriam exspectant.
15. Cura vaccas, o filia.
16. Nautam iuvamus.
17. Copiae fossam intrant.
18. Patriam conservatis.
19. Explora viam.
20. Pecuniam exspectamus.
21. Victoria nautas excitat.
22. Sagittasne vitatis?
23. Arate, o agricolae.
24. Praeda copias delectat.
25. Nautae fortunam culpant.
26. Nonne deam laudas?
27. Exspecta epistolam.
28. Num patriam vitas?
29. Procella terram vastat.
30. Quo properant nautae?

EXERCISE 173 (Chapters 1–5)

1. The land delights farmers.
2. The sailors carry water.
3. Call the cow, my daughter.
4. Fortune helps the farmer.
5. The girls look after cows.
6. We are ploughing the land.
7. Free your country, sailors.
8. The queen calls the troops.
9. The island delights the girl.
10. They are building a hut.
11. Is he not approaching?
12. The cows enter the road.
13. You are freeing the island.
14. Surely he does not swim?
15. The farmer cuts hay.
16. We seize the road.
17. Enter the island.
18. He waits for the troops.
19. A storm approaches.
20. Wait for the battle.
21. They demand water.
22. Why do you hurry?
23. The troops free their land.
24. I do not blame fortune.
25. Does he demand money?
26. The wood hides the moon.
27. Farmers plough the land.
28. We wait for victory.
29. Do you dread storms?
30. We love our country.

EXERCISE 174 (Chapters 6–10)

1. Incolae oram Britanniae vitant.
2. Statua deae puellas delectat.
3. Cur pecuniam nautis datis?
4. Turbam incolarum hastis fugamus.
5. Nautae a Britannia navigant.
6. Victoriam nautarum incolis nuntiamus.
7. Puellae cum agricola laborant.
8. Caesar copias e silva revocat.
9. Amicitia incolarum nautas delectat.
10. Ante pugnam hastas parant.
11. Victoriam nauta reginae nuntiat.
12. In silvas incolas fugate.
13. Caesar in fossa copias celat.
14. Cur contra patriam pugnatis?
15. Victoriamne nautae deam orant?

EXERCISE 175 (Chapters 6–10)

1. The anger of the queen rouses the troops.
2. The natives attack with spears.
3. Hurry from the wood to the road.
4. We give water to the sailors.
5. The Druids live in the wood.
6. The farmer's daughter is ploughing the land.
7. Ask the sailor his opinion.
8. We are sailing from Athens to Rome.
9. The shore of their native land delights the sailors.
10. Boadicea is hurrying with her troops.
11. We show the booty to the sailors.
12. Caesar ravages the land with flames.
13. The eagles fly into the wood.
14. We dread the natives' spears.
15. Why do you not live in Rome?

EXERCISE 176 (Chapters 11–15)

1. Fortuna victoriam Druidis non dabit.
2. Hastas, non sagittas, parabamus.
3. Caesar in Britannia non diu manet.
4. Copias magnas Britannorum timebamus.
5. Dominus bonus servos bene curabat.
6. Bellum longum Britannis non placebat.
7. Nostri hastas longas in dextris habebant.
8. Magister noster pueros non terrebit.
9. Romani pro populo libero pugnabant.
10. Post victoriam magnam nostri ad castra appropinquant.
11. Nauta bonus stellas saepe spectat.
12. Fabulam pulchram filiae nostrae narrabo.
13. Nostri signo praefecti non parebant.
14. Fabri barbarorum gladios ad bellum parant.
15. Multos amicos Londinii videbimus.

EXERCISE 177 (Chapters 11–15)

1. The master will give a small reward to the good boy.
2. We are staying in a beautiful island.
3. The Britons were fighting near the shore.
4. The commander was encouraging our men with a few words.
5. Many dangers frightened our troops.
6. The allies began to build small forts.
7. Obey the advice of your commander.
8. The wretched prisoners were lying on rough stones.
9. Many were hiding their goods in a thick wood.
10. Good farmers look after their slaves.
11. The master will teach the boys many languages.
12. We will not destroy the beautiful town.
13. On the ground was lying a long spear.
14. We will not wait for our allies.
15. The slaves will not work for their master today.

EXERCISE 178 (Chapters 16–20)

1. Fossa Romanorum erat alta et lata.
2. Erat Londinii magnum dei templum.
3. Milites in oppido Deva manebant.
4. Est Androclo amicus bonus.
5. In Britannia, insula pulchra, habitamus.
6. Hercules leonem saevum tandem necavit.
7. Ubi stas, fuit quondam oppidum.
8. Romani Romulum, regem primum, in numero deorum habebant.
9. Dux magna voce pedites revocavit.
10. Ubi Britannos superaveritis, ad Galliam navigabitis.
11. Consules Romani viam non exploraverant.
12. Pauci equites duci supererant.
13. Patremne de periculo monuisti?
14. Consulibus, non regi, nunc paremus.
15. Milites vocem ducis non timuerunt.

EXERCISE 179 (Chapters 16–20)

1. The walls of the town were thick.
2. Your words will be welcome to the people.
3. We are sailing to Britain, a distant province.
4. You will be far from the town of London.
5. Caesar had sailed with his infantry to Britain.
6. The soldiers were not in great danger.
7. The inhabitants had been afraid of the lion for a long time.
8. The boys obeyed their master's voice.
9. When we have swum, we will have dinner.
10. The commander had trained cavalry for the king.
11. My father feared the voices of the robbers.
12. The infantry have new shields.
13. Hurry from the ditch when I shout.
14. The soldiers have hurried into the wood with their leader.
15. A fierce lion had walked into the circus.

EXERCISE 184 (Chapters 31–34)

1. Galli tria oppida deleverunt.
2. Implete duas amphoras vino.
3. Pedites flumen intrare timebant.
4. Multos dies in ea urbe mansimus.
5. Equites Caesarem in proelio non adiuverunt.
6. Circum insulam septem dies navigabamus.
7. Duobus diebus Athenas perveneris.
8. Britanni hostibus resistere constituerunt.
9. Non erat facile Romanis Gallos superare.
10. Num hieme in flumine natare audes?
11. Nolite consilium senum neglegere.
12. Et boves et sues agricola curabat.
13. Senibus non satis est virium.
14. Quarto die castra ad flumen movimus.
15. In virtute spem habete, o milites.

EXERCISE 185 (Chapters 31–34)

1. We reached the town on the third day.
2. The infantry remained there in vain for many hours.
3. Not even old men were afraid to fight for their country.
4. We shall have destroyed the city within two hours.
5. Both rich and poor hastened to defend the city.
6. The journey was long for the old men.
7. It was difficult for the prisoner to reply.
8. Don't help the enemy.
9. The force of the storm delayed the ships.
10. On the next day we advanced to the river.
11. The state is no longer in danger.
12. Farmers are accustomed to work for many hours.
13. The boy learnt to swim in five days.
14. To neglect good friends is disgraceful.
15. The Britons gave a pledge to the Romans.

EXERCISE 186 (Miscellaneous)

1. Milites se a catenis liberaverunt.
2. Nemo e captivis imperatori respondit.
3. Dux magna voce suos ad arma revocavit.
4. Non suos, sed amici libros puer portat.
5. Pars mari, pars terra venerunt.
6. Nubes nigra a sinistra apparuerat.
7. Multa bella Romani contra hostes gesserunt.
8. Pueri verba magistri non intellexerant.
9. Iuvenes a consilio audaci non destiterunt.
10. Cur tot annos hic mansisti?
11. Hostes pontem rumpere iam constituerant.
12. Caesar praedam militibus post proelium dedit.
13. Nolite foedus rumpere.
14. Toti exercitui Caesar praeerat.
15. Filio meo et amicis eius ianuam aperiam.

EXERCISE 187 (Miscellaneous)

1. We found our dog on the third day.
2. My friends and I stayed in the country for three days.
3. Lead the cavalry towards the mountain without delay.
4. The city of Rome was once on fire.
5. We determined to attack the enemy before night.
6. The Romans obeyed one general, the Gauls many.
7. Why are the Britons fighting each other?
8. Do not climb the mountain today.
9. Surely our men will not give themselves up to the enemy?
10. Young men were accustomed to ask him for his opinion.
11. Caesar decided to hurry from Rome to Gaul.
12. It is difficult to guard against all dangers.
13. The general advanced and did not hesitate to attack.
14. Why did his sons not remain in Athens?
15. Soon you will read the second book.